## Contents

*Critical Guides to French Texts*

45  Du Bellay: Poems

*Critical Guides to French Texts*

EDITED BY ROGER LITTLE, WOLFGANG VAN EMDEN, DAVID WILLIAMS

DU BELLAY

# Poems

Kathleen M. Hall

Senior Lecturer in French,
University of Southampton

and

Margaret B. Wells

Grant & Cutler Ltd
1985

© Grant & Cutler Ltd
1985
ISBN 0 7293 0217 2

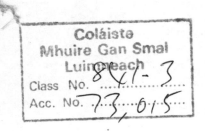
I.S.B.N. 84-599-0402-4

DEPÓSITO LEGAL: V. 297 - 1985

Printed in Spain by
Artes Gráficas Soler, S.A., Valencia
for
GRANT & CUTLER LTD
11 BUCKINGHAM STREET, LONDON W.C.2

## *Preface*

This book concentrates on Du Bellay's major poetic collections: *L'Olive* of 1549-50 with the accompanying 'Vers lyriques', and the three French collections published in 1558 following his return from Rome. For convenience, references are to H. Chamard's edition of his complete works, since the series being published by Droz (Textes Littéraires Français) is not yet complete. Details of the volumes so far published in that series will be found in the Select Bibliography at the end of this volume; figures in italics refer to items as numbered in this.

At various points, mentioned in footnotes, use is made of material already published in *French Studies*, *Forum for Modern Language Studies* and *Modern Language Review*. We thank the editors for their permission to re-use this material.

# 1. Introduction

Du Bellay nowhere gives a precise definition of poetry; perhaps to do so is impossible. In his first and most provocative publication, *La Deffence et illustration de la langue françoyse*, he describes the great classical poets as surpassing prose writers

> à cause de ceste divinité d'invention qu'ilz ont plus que les autres, de ceste grandeur de style, magnificence de motz, gravité de sentences, audace & varieté de figures, & mil' autres lumieres de poësie: bref ceste energie, & ne scay quel esprit, qui est en leurs ecriz, que les Latins appelleroient *genius*. (I,6)

Evidently poetry is a form of expression so elevated above prose as to become something indescribably different. It is achieved by 'ceste ardeur & allegresse d'esprit qui naturellement excite les poëtes', but also requires hard work, 'suer & trembler maintesfois ... endurer de faim, de soif & de longues vigiles' (II,3). He describes his own aim as 'une nouvelle poësie' (II,1) unexplained there, but explained in the preface to the second edition of the *Olive* (see chapter 3) as 'une nouvelle, ou plustost ancienne renouvelée poësie' in which effects would be gained through 'l'immitation des anciens Latins & des poëtes Italiens'. He goes on in that preface, however, to claim that in his poems 'y a beaucoup plus de naturelle invention que d'artificielle ou supersticieuse [ = over-scrupulous] immitation'.

But one must remember what Grahame Castor (*20*, pp.86 ff.) points out, that 'invention' in the sixteenth century did not mean imagination. It was a process less of 'making' than of 'finding' — seeking out and selecting appropriate material, both concepts to be communicated and methods of communicating them, ways of persuading the reader to react appropriately. It included even the use of borrowings, the choice of the right Latin or Italian

poem to be used as model, of the right Greek or Latin tag to be
rendered in French; and when Du Bellay or Ronsard quoted in
this way, he was showing sound but not exceptional erudition.

A Renaissance writer, even a Renaissance reader, had received
an education with a marked bias towards the classical, theo-
retical and encyclopaedic. He had a thorough knowledge of
Latin, and some Greek. He had at least a smattering, perhaps a
good deal more, of mathematics and science, geography and
astronomy, philosophy and theology; if it was not often first-
hand knowledge based on experience, yet it could be an
extensive acquaintance with what had been said on the subject
by the greatest classical authors and their most modern
commentators. As well as of learning, his mind was full of
symbolism, in the mediaeval tradition again revivified and
enriched by the classics, which were read both in the original and
with the help of emblem-books and encyclopaedias of
mythology; Diana for him was at once the goddess of the moon,
hunting and chastity, and, as Hecate, a goddess of night, death
and the underworld — a very powerful combination of
associations. He had had a long training in logic, rhetoric or
both, the arts of distinguishing concepts clearly and putting
them over effectively; and once again, for him, it was the great
classics who were the masters of these arts. Under their
guidance, out of this mass of material, the writer could choose,
and the reader could appreciate, the right concept for any
moment or context, conveyed by an appropriate vehicle of
quotation or commonplace, allusion or imagery.

After 'invention', as Du Bellay himself explains in the
*Deffence* (I,5), came 'eloquution', the choice of words them-
selves, and 'disposition', the choice of the right order for one's
concepts, devices and words. But these too were not left entirely
to individual subjective reactions; there was a stock of
recommended media and tools, for instance the universally
accepted idea of the three styles of writing, high (or 'grand'),
middle, and low (simple and everyday rather than vulgar or
grotesque, although this last style existed too). Particular
traditions had their own traditional languages, such as the
hyperboles of court compliment or the images and antitheses of

Petrarchism, and their own traditional set verse-forms, in the former case the long poem in rhyming couplets, in the latter case the sonnet. The choice and use of any of these resources did not imply artificiality or insincerity; Renaissance writers were craftsmen, using materials and methods appropriate to their purpose with integrity and, sometimes, inspiration. They were becoming steadily more conscious of the significative power of individual words and epithets, 'de sorte, que sans eux ce que tu diras seroit beaucoup moindre', as the *Deffence* put it (II,9); and, with developments in music towards 'a greater picturesqueness',[1] 'more related to human feelings',[2] they were becoming highly sensitive to the appeal of poetry to the ear. Rhyme, for example, said the *Deffence* (II,7), 'ne contentera moins l'oreille, qu'une bien armonieuse musique tumbante en un bon & parfait accord'.

It was in April 1549 that Du Bellay published *La Deffence* together with *L'Olive*, a collection of love-sonnets which was itself accompanied by a collection of 'Vers lyriques'. The elements of poetic style presented to the public in these volumes, in theory or by example, were not new in themselves; Clément Marot had been an equally polished craftsman, Maurice Scève was an equally subtle exploiter of the learning of his time; and poems had already been published by Ronsard, Du Bellay's comrade-in-arms, and Peletier, an older member of the group of friends which Ronsard was to call the 'Pléiade'. But Du Bellay rises above his predecessors, and, with Ronsard, leads their followers, firstly by his demand for a serious aim and high standard:

j'ay tousjours estimé notre poësie Francoyse estre capable
de quelque plus hault & meilleur style que celuy dont nous
sommes si longuement contentez ... (II,1)

secondly by his emphasis on a strong emotive effect even in light poetry:

[1] Bruce Pattison, *Music and Poetry of the English Renaissance*, London: Methuen, 1948, p.100.

[2] *New Oxford History of Music*, vol.III, Oxford University Press, 1960, p.217.

celuy sera veritablement le poëte que je cherche en nostre
Langue, qui me fera indigner, apayser, ejouyr, douloir,
aymer, hayr, admirer, etonner, bref, qui tiendra la bride de
mes affections, me tournant ça & la à son plaisir. (II,11)

At the end of the second preface to the *Olive*, however, he
gives a place also to the right of individual expression, the right
of the poet to choose his own approach and suit the taste of
some readers if not of others:

J'ay tousjours estimé la poësie comme ung somptueux
banquet, ou chacun est le bien venu, & n'y force lon
personne de manger d'une viande ou boire d'un vin, s'il
n'est à son goust ...

We shall find the great characteristics of Du Bellay's poetic
work to be the variety and richness appropriate to such a
banquet. A technique of sonnet-writing which he himself
developed in French, in the *Olive* and his other love-poetry,
reaches its perfection in the very different sequences of the
*Antiquitez* and the *Regrets*; so does a method of handling
universal and philosophical issues which is to be seen in germ in
the odes which accompanied and followed the *Olive*. The lighter
*Divers jeux rustiques*, the third collection of his peak period,
returns, though not in sonnet form, to the *Olive*'s and the odes'
themes of love and compliment and to the satirical vein of the
*Regrets*, while also bringing to a climax his experiments in trans-
lation and imitation.

## 2. A Short Chapter on Metre

Musical and emotive effects can be achieved in French poetry not only, as in English, through rhythm, the pattern of stressed and unstressed syllables, and tempo, the pattern of quick and slow syllables, phrases and pauses; but also, as in French prose speech, by pitch, the pattern of high and low tones, and even, as in Latin, by quantity, the pattern of long and short syllables. To all this a mere background is provided by metre, the system of rules governing a strict verse form or line. An understanding of metre is necessary for the appreciation of the rhythm and music of any formal verse, and especially French verse; but the basic rules are not difficult.

(1) Where a line of strict English verse, for example a Shakespearian pentameter, has a fixed number of stresses but can have extra unstressed syllables,

His scéptre shóws the fórce of témp(o)ral pówer,

a strict French line must have a fixed and correct number of syllables; if it did not, it would have been considered such a mistake before the days of free verse that a good poet would not have published it. Syllables are counted in the same way whatever the length of a line; but we shall illustrate from one of Du Bellay's best-known sonnets (*Regrets*, 31), written in alexandrines (lines of twelve syllables):

Heureux qui comm(e) Ulyss(e) a fait un beau voyag(e) ...

(2) The *e*'s of 'comm(e)' and 'Ulyss(e)' were elided in Du Bellay's time, as now, disappearing into the following vowel. But in the next line,

Ou comme cestuy là qui conquit la toison,

the *e* of 'comme', which would now be unpronounced and called mute or neutral, would in classical French verse be called feminine, counted in scansion and even lightly pronounced; 'comme' would be heard as not very different from the English 'comma'. This applied to all unelided 'mute' *e*'s, whether at the end of a word followed by a word beginning with a consonant, before the end of a word ('p*e*tit'), after an acute *é* ('cheminee*') or at the end of a line ('voyag*e*'). The Comédie Française still pronounces a syllable followed by a feminine *e* as slightly longer than one not so followed, and the audience senses the syllables as slightly different. If Du Bellay had carelessly offered 'cheminee' as a rhyme for 'retourné' the error would have been condemned in his own time, and would even now be somewhat disturbing to a French ear.

Strictly it might be said that the final *e* of 'voyage' gives thirteen syllables to the first line of the sonnet, and indeed in Du Bellay's time the alexandrine was often called a 'vers de douze à treize sillabes'; but the normal thing now is to speak of a masculine or feminine alexandrine. It must be remembered that these terms, when used of rhyme, simply mean without or with the final *e*, and have nothing to do with grammatical gender; 'la toison' has a masculine ending, 'un beau voyage' a feminine one.

(3) Two vowels in hiatus make two syllables, as in 'audac*ieu*x', which has four syllables in all; 'voyage', as has been seen, has three. But a diphthong counts as a single syllable; 'toison' has two syllables only, 'ardoise' three only. (It should be noted that this diphthong was pronounced [wɛ] or [ɛ] in Du Bellay's time, in these words as well as in 'revoiray-je', 'Loyre' and 'Gaulois'. This will often mean that a poem is less full of harsh sounds than might be thought.)

But all this does not mean that an alexandrine was or is pronounced or heard as a series of twelve bonks or six ke-bonks.[3] Even Shakespeare's decasyllabic line would never be delivered as

[3] Marjorie Boulton, *The Anatomy of Poetry*, London: Routledge & Kegan Paul, 1982, p.28 et seq. See also H.E. Berthon, *Nine French Poets*, London: Macmillan, 1945, introduction, for a full and simple account of the versification of classical French.

scanned above; an actor will give a lighter emphasis to 'shows' than to 'scep(tre)', perhaps a stronger one to 'force', probably the strongest to 'temp(oral)'. French has always stressed the twelfth syllable of an alexandrine, and, until Victor Hugo's time, the sixth; but, in Du Bellay's line, 'heureux' may be stressed on its second or, emotionally, on its first syllable; 'comme Ulysse', as a parenthesis, will perhaps be dropped to a lower pitch, certainly with no stress on 'comme'; 'beau', with another strong emotional stress, may well be slightly lengthened either in respect of its own quantity or by an almost imperceptible pause after it. It is because of the controlling force of the twelve-syllable structure behind the alexandrine that such variations can be practised and appreciated without the danger of collapse into prose.

Theoretically a French metrical line may be of any length, and occasionally Du Bellay amused himself by writing three- or five-syllable lines. In practice, these were rarely used, nine- or eleven-syllable lines even more rarely before the nineteenth century. The serious or 'heroic' line was the decasyllable; lighter verse commonly used the octosyllable, sometimes the six- or seven-syllable line; if a stanza combined lines of varied lengths, they were most often hexa-, octo- or decasyllables. It was Du Bellay and Ronsard themselves who glimpsed the rich possibilities of the alexandrine, although at first a little uncertainly; Ronsard was to explain in his *Abbregé de l'art poetique* (1565) that its length compared to that of the decasyllable ran the risk of suggesting prose: 'et sentiroyent la prose, si n'estoyent composez de motz esleus, graves, et resonnans, et d'une ryme assez riche, afin que telle richesse empesche le stille de la prose' (*27*, XIV, 25). However, taking such precautions, the Pléiade made the alexandrine into the most beautiful line of French verse.

The alexandrine was also saved from an indeterminacy which might render it prosaic by the rule that it must have a pause in the sound and a break between sense-groups, not only after the twelfth but also after the sixth syllable, where it is called a caesura as in Latin. Decasyllables had a similar pause after the fourth syllable; it is probably pointless to seek for caesurae in shorter lines. Sometimes the caesura is not the major pause in the line; one might claim that in

  Revoiray-je le clos de ma pauvre maison ...

the break before 'le clos' is more marked than that after it; but
before the nineteenth century the caesura never disappeared
completely. In any period, however, one may find *enjambe-
ment*, the flowing on of the sense from the end of one verse line
to the beginning of the next, with the result that the end-pause
becomes less prominent than the following caesura:

                              ... de ma pauvre maison
  Qui m'est une province ...

*Enjambement*, too, may be less or more marked, and many
critics confine the use of the term to passages where the first line,
such as

  Quand revoiray-je, helas! de mon petit village ...

would be meaningless without what follows, or to passages
where the overflow consists of less than half a line:

  O combien (dy-je alors) la grandeur que je voy
  Est miserable / au pris de la grandeur d'un Roy!
                                        (*Regrets*, 118)

Such *enjambement* can have a strong effect of surprise or
emphasis.

  Theoretically, also, a stanza may be of any length, and of any
pattern, but again some have been more popular at different
periods. Long narrative or reflective poems are most often com-
posed in couplets, where the rhyme satisfies the ear without,
usually, drawing special attention to itself; Du Bellay follows
this tradition. Before his time eight-line stanzas were very
popular, especially if rhyming *ababbcbc*, where each letter of the
alphabet indicates a different rhyme-sound (the Ulysses sonnet
would be recorded as rhyming *abba abba ccd eed*). A pretty

pattern, occasionally used earlier, is that which Ronsard brought
to perfection in 'Bel aubepin...' Lines 1, 3, 4 and 6 are of seven
syllables, lines 2 and 5 of three, while the rhyme-scheme is *aab
ccb*; Du Bellay used this stanza in three poems. The form which
he and his colleagues loved and popularized most, however, was
the sonnet.

It is probably a mistake for a beginner to attempt to read a
Renaissance sonnet-sequence at a sitting. The sonnets should be
savoured separately and slowly, perhaps no more than two or
three at a time, and later re-read as elements in a larger compo-
sition. The total structure will then become apparent and in its
turn permit a deeper appreciation of each poem.

A sonnet is not simply a poem of fourteen lines, all (at least in
Du Bellay's times) of the same length. The essential and exciting
thing is that any subdivision of fourteen lines must be an
unequal one (no-one would give the name of sonnet to a poem of
seven couplets or of two seven-line stanzas). Shakespeare used a
12:2 subdivision; the Italian and French tradition was to use an
8:6 one. In either case, the earlier part of the sonnet has more
space, is more leisurely, exploratory or reflective; the latter part
changes tempo, speeds up, hastens to its goal with more con-
centration and intensity. This change of tempo may be
sharpened if the first eight lines (the octave) are clearly divided
into two quatrains which balance each other, the last six (the
sestet) into two tercets of which the first may fulfil much the
same role as one or both quatrains, the second a quite different
role. Of course this is not the only way of exploiting the octave;
and the sestet can be divided in many different ways, $2+4$ or
$4+2$ as well as $3+3$, even $5+1$ or some other arrangement.
Further, the rhyme pattern, although usually *abba abba* in the
octave, can also vary widely in the sestet, either reinforcing the
sense or forming a counterpoint in subtle contrast with it.

The sestet may employ either two or three rhyme-sounds,
which should not be those of the octave. In theory this permits
twenty-four sestet-patterns; but tradition rules out some of
these. To rhyme the first and last line of a sestet (lines 9 and 14
of the sonnet) is thought to keep the reader or hearer too long in
suspense; to rhyme the last two lines, as Shakespeare does

always and as Ronsard and Du Bellay do on occasions, is
thought by the French to have a flat and sententious effect.
Other patterns are excluded by the rule, which Ronsard and Du
Bellay slowly evolved in the 1550s, that a poet should observe
*alternance* of masculine and feminine rhymes; that is, no two
*different* masculine rhymes may ever be adjacent, and similarly
no two feminine ones. If a poem is written in couplets, the
second must be of the opposite gender from the first and third.
Where masculine and feminine lines interweave otherwise, still
the rule must be observed; if the *a*-rhyme of a sonnet is
masculine, the *b*-rhyme must be feminine, and the *c*-rhyme also
feminine, since it will be adjacent in line 9 to a masculine line 8.
So the sestet *cde cde*, beloved by the Italians, becomes illegiti-
mate in French; if the *c*-rhyme were feminine and the *d*-rhyme
masculine, what could the *e*-rhyme be? It must be repeated that
for the French this is not meaningless pedantry; the difference in
the quality of the rhymes is to them audible and harmonious, the
lack of it audible, discordant and distasteful.

    Further complications can ensue if the rule of *alternance* is to
be observed in lyrics composed in stanzas or strophes.[4] These
will be discussed in the note which follows. But where the rule is
perfectly obeyed, as in the best of the *Divers jeux rustiques*, it
contributes much to the musical effect.

*Note on 'alternance' in strophic writing*

    *Alternance* was the systematized logical development of the
type of arrangement of masculine and feminine lines with which
Du Bellay had experimented initially in the 1549 'Vers lyriques'.
Although in all of these odes Du Bellay maintained regular
rhyme-schemes, in most of them he did not arrange masculine
and feminine lines according to particular patterns. But in Odes
2 and 5 the changes in rhyme are matched by changes in rhyme
gender — and it is this sort of arrangement which is now known
as *alternance*. Odes 7 and 9 represent a half-way position which
did not establish itself in French classical versification, and for

---

[4] There is no difference between these two terms — the use of either avoids the
ambiguity which might result from the use of 'verse'.

which we propose the new name of gender-patterning: both the rhyme-scheme and the arrangement of masculine and feminine endings follow those set out in the initial strophe, but two different masculine (or feminine) rhymes are to be found in juxtaposition. In all these four odes, however, every strophe in a particular poem can be superimposed on the first one.[5]

In the 1550 *Recueil de poësie* stricter arrangements can be seen. Twelve odes show fully regular *alternance*. Because of the metre chosen by Du Bellay, the *alternance* in the 'Prosphonematique' and in Ode 13 is only 'intra-strophic':[6] i.e. the final rhyme-word of a strophe is 'odd' (*a, c, e, g,* etc.) and the strophe begins and ends with a rhyme of the same gender. This leads to the disturbing of the regular alternation of the masculine and feminine rhymes within the poem as a whole.[7] A mere three odes (3, 7 and 11) display only gender-patterning. Nevertheless, in each ode in this collection, there is some type of regular pattern of masculine and feminine lines which allows subsequent strophes to be superimposed on the first one.

A further incomplete type of *alternance*, which we call 'interstrophic', occurs when the number of rhymes in a strophe is such as to permit the succession of masculine and feminine rhymes to proceed smoothly throughout the poem as a whole, but to make them fall in a different place within successive strophes. An example is 'Aux dames angevines' (appended to *L'Olive augmentee*), where each strophe has three pairs of rhymes; odd strophes begin with a feminine rhyme and even ones with a masculine one. Thus successive strophes cannot be superimposed on the first. Only when the *alternance* is both intra- and inter-strophic can it be termed fully regular.

Although it was only in the 1549 'Vers lyriques' that Du

---

[5] The musical necessity for this is still a controversial issue. See B. Jeffery, 'The idea of music in Ronsard's poetry', in *Ronsard the Poet*, ed. T. Cave, London: Methuen, 1973, pp.211-14.

[6] Our use of this term differs slightly from Laumonier's (*Ronsard, poète lyrique*, Paris: Hachette, 1909, pp.669 ff.).

[7] 'La Musagnœomachie', 'Immitation d'une ode latine de Jan Dorat', 'Contre les envieux poëtes', 'La Lyre chrestienne', and 'Les Deux Marguerites' all show intra-strophic *alternance* (*1*, IV).

Bellay, 'craignant de contraindre et de gehinner [sa] diction', shunned a regular arrangement of line genders, he did not rush to adopt fully regular *alternance*. Examples of intra-strophic *alternance* and of gender-patterning can be found quite frequently up to 1552, the latter even as late as 1557/8 (in the *chanson* 'Tristes souspirs', *1*, V, p.391). Gender-patterning also, of course, occurs in some of Du Bellay's sonnets (e.g. *L'Olive*, 1, 3, 5, 10, 12, etc.), although in general he accepted that no two different masculine (or two different feminine) lines should be adjacent.

## 3. 'L'Olive': Sonnets on Love

To express emotion through conventions, traditions, learned imagery and set verse-forms perhaps seems most unnatural when the emotion is that of love. 'From one point of view', says Marjorie Boulton, 'much love poetry is the expression of besotted idealizations; but', she continues, 'love-poems may also be seen as verbal presents made in tenderness, a refinement of wooing, an offering of skills to one's beloved'.[8] Besides, a Renaissance poet was concerned not with his own auto-biography, but with what was universal in his experience, real or fancied. Selecting a real or imagined woman as the focus for feelings perceived in himself or conceived as possible, he hoped that like-minded readers or listeners would accept his words as expressing the inarticulate emotions of any wooer, the imperfectly sensitive reactions of anyone being wooed. There is no evidence as to the existence of a real lady (whatever her name) with whom Du Bellay was in love; but his first sequence of love-sonnets is much more than a mere competent exercise.

Rather than the arrogant approach which Ronsard was to develop — 'aimés moy, ce pendant qu'estes belle'[9] — Du Bellay adopted the more insinuating attitude derived from mediaeval courtly love, but by his time known as 'petrarchizing' from the name of its most famous exponent. The lover exaggerates his sense of unworthiness, admits the beloved's right to reserve, coldness and caprice, but emphasizes his humble appreciation of her qualities, his readiness to 'serve', oblige and entertain, and his frustrations at an unresponsiveness which can be termed ingratitude. The approach is made into more than a mere technique of courtship by Petrarch's vivid perception of the

[8] *The Anatomy of Literary Studies*, London: Routledge & Kegan Paul, 1980, p.148.

[9] *Continuation des Amours* (1555), sonnet 35; ed. Laumonier (*27*) VII, pp.152-53.

psychology of the lover and of the sensitizing power of love, and by his development of an effective repertoire of poetic devices to communicate his insights. His followers, including Du Bellay, enriched their poetry by imitating his, and often by associating with his psychology and aesthetic what these already contained in germ, a version of Plato's philosophy more or less coloured by Christianity: learning how to appreciate truth and beauty, especially moral and spiritual, and how to love in an increasingly sensitive and unselfish way, purifies the soul, assists it to escape from the debasing influence of the merely physical and to rise to union with God and likeness to Him. Helpful accounts of Renaissance Petrarchism and Neoplatonism are given by Vianey (*31*), Chamard (*21*), Weber (*32*) and Merrill and Clements (*29*).[10]

\*    \*    \*

Those who claim to see no 'différence sérieuse' (Chamard, *21*, I, p.223) between the *Olive* of 1549, of fifty sonnets,[11] and the expanded version of 1550, seem never to have considered the original sequence as one complete in its own right. Like other Renaissance sonnet-sequences, it does not attempt to tell a clear and continuous story; the sonnets are not stills from a film or even cartoons from a strip; but, as in other sequences, each sonnet portrays some aspect of love or mood of the lover, finally arranged into an order with a beginning, a progress and a climax. After reading *L'Olive* as it first appeared, one may then turn to the later interpolations (the sonnets finally numbered 23, 32, 40, 44, 46, 50, 53, 56 and 58) and additions (60 onwards), and appreciate how they enrich the earlier sequence, exploit old and new themes, and continue to an unexpected conclusion.

[10] And also by A.M.J. Festugière, *La Philosophie de l'amour de Marcile Ficin et son influence sur la littérature française au XVI<sup>e</sup> siècle*, Revista da universidade de Coimbra, 1922; Paris: Etudes de philosophie médiévale, 1941; Nesca A. Robb, *Neoplatonism of the Italian Renaissance*, London: Allen & Unwin, 1935, and L.W. Forster, *The Icy Fire*, Cambridge University Press, 1969. Meanwhile Demerson (*24*) will be valuable on mythology in the *Olive*, and Griffin (*12*) on the logical and rhetorical structure of many of the sonnets.

[11] References to sonnets in this sequence will use the numbering of the later expanded edition.

The first *Olive* begins, and ends in what became Sonnet 59, with Du Bellay's assertion of his aim to immortalize his lady, and himself as her lover. Sonnet 1, introducing the first original sonnet-sequence to appear in France, and adorned with a continuous accompaniment of allusion, must have had an impact in 1549 like nothing before, except perhaps Scève's 1544 sequence of dixains to 'Délie'. Characteristically self-deprecating, Du Bellay disclaims the desire to attain prophetic, mystical or even erotic frenzy,[12] inspired by Apollo, Bacchus or Venus; his ambition is for the gift of Pallas Athene, the olive-wreath which symbolizes peace and wisdom, virginity (according to Dorothy Coleman, *9*, pp.29-30) and (according to Françoise Joukovsky, *26*, pp.381-82) divine mercy and the promise of immortality. The use of the octave of a sonnet to make these disclaimers suggests also, initially, an intention not to rival Petrarch; the sestet with its references to laurel, Petrarch's symbol, makes clear his intention to do exactly that; and the ease with which the ideas glide into mellifluous lines, well-rhymed and only discreetly inverted, goes far beyond what Clément Marot and other earlier sonneteers had achieved. The almost casual references and epithets, full of meaning to the ear attuned to the classics, strike the keynote of the whole sequence; and between the negations and the prayers rings out a prophecy of his destiny as a Palladian poet, 'le ciel me l'ordonne', as confident as any of Ronsard's.

Sonnet 2 is a free translation from an Italian source, as are nearly twenty others in the sequence; Sonnet 3 was inspired, like some fifteen others, by an Italian suggestion. Yet both are well calculated to show how Olive has been divinely created and endowed to reflect the qualities of her patron goddess, and to increase the latter's renown and that of her own birthplace, as 3 adds with the characteristic patriotism of the Pléiade. Olive's only inconsistency, 4 and 5 reveal, is her 'cruelty' towards her lover. He cannot praise her enough (6-10); what surprises him in the last line of Sonnet 7 is not, of course, his mere faithfulness to such a paragon, but his endurance of the torture of frustrated

[12] See Pontus de Tyard, *Le Solitaire premier*, 1552; or H. Franchet, *Le Poète et son œuvre d'après Ronsard*, Paris: Champion, 1923.

love for her. Yet she alone (seen as Venus in Sonnet 11 line 11, and perhaps also, there and in Sonnet 12, as the Virgin Mary, Star of the Sea) saves him from despair and death (11-12). His dream of embracing her is an illusion; dreams which come to one through ivory gates, according to Homer and Virgil, are fallacious. But his constant and fervent love will immortalize her and him (13, etc.).

These themes intertwine throughout the fifty sonnets, where classical and Italian borrowings are aptly remembered and skilfully arranged to build up the picture of the beloved as the incarnation of all natural beauty and all supernatural gifts. Sonnets 15 to 22 continue to concentrate on this; Sonnets 24 onwards return to the subject, introduced briefly in 4-5 and 7-8, of her lover's suffering. This is not to be seen as mere wallowing in self-pity, but as an additional way of praising her; the greater the lady's elevation above all others, the greater the frustration of the mere mortal who has set his heart on the unattainable. The most touching sonnet of the fifty is perhaps 45, picturing in grisaille the rejected lover's desolation in a world radiant with love, the loves of Jupiter and Juno, Uranus (Heaven) and Gæa (Earth), Zephyrus and the bird-shaped Podarge, Venus and Adonis or Apollo and Hyacinthus. But Sonnets 29 and 33-42 have reasserted the poet's constancy and hope, and hinted that his experiences inspire and ennoble him:

Qu'en moy soudain un feu divin s'assemble,
Qui mue, altere & ravist ma nature.  (38)

The sequence closes with prayers for mercy, invoking in turn Sleep and Death (47), Ocean and all nature (48-49, 54), the reader (51), Venus (52), Love (55) and Olive herself; her graces and his torments are alike innumerable (57), but, dying like Leander and descending to hell like Æneas (59), he will bring back the golden bough of her fame.

Even by 1549 Du Bellay had discovered the sonnet form to be not constricting but exciting. The sonnets of the *Antiquitez* and *Regrets* were to be his masterpieces; but already in the first *Olive* he exploited the symmetry produced by uniform line-length; the reader's expectation of a memorable fourteenth line (Sonnet 2) perhaps carrying a surprising or epigrammatic punch (7); the possibility of constructing a whole sonnet from a single sentence (13), changing tempo sharply after the octave (9), or breaking both octave and sestet clearly into quatrains and tercets (16). Some thirty of the fifty sonnets divide the sestet evenly; but others split it into 4 + 2 lines (28, 30), 2 + 4 (41), even 1 + 5 (9) or three couplets (7, 14, 39, 55). The regular *abba abba* rhyme-scheme of the octave can emphasize tense (18) or femininity (39). The freer rhyme-scheme of the sestet may echo the meaning, as in 12, where Olive, the 'amyable' and 'pitoyable', can alone 'terminer' and 'illuminer' the author's 'ame offensée' and 'triste pensée'; or it may play against it in clever counterpoint, as when Sonnet 13 affirms that the poet's mental image of Olive, 'le protraict' of 'beautez ... nées' and 'figure ... peinte', will never be destroyed by the very concepts that provide the required rhymes, 'années', 'eau ... ceinte' and the poppy 'qui le sommeil attraict'.

The rule of *alternance* had not yet evolved: one of Du Bellay's first sonnets (7) is entirely in feminine rhymes; several more have feminine octaves; others (5, 10, 15, 41) make effective use of the Italian sestet *cde cde*. Only half the 1549 sestets are in the forms which were to become the most popular French ones, *ccd eed* (9 sonnets) and *ccd ede* (16 sonnets). Even so, content and form can be matched to varied effect, in the precise symmetry of a *ccd eed* structure (20) or the thought-provoking openness of a closed *cc* couplet followed by a new departure, *deed* (49) or *dede* (17). Together with end-stopped lines one finds dramatic *enjambements* (9, second quatrain; 21, 30, 48). Finally one may note two sonnets, 10 and 19, in the bizarre but powerful form of 'vers rapportés', apparently introduced into French by Du Bellay himself (but to be used still more strikingly by Jodelle in his 'Des astres, des forests, et d'Acheron ...'). Different images, usually three in number, are systematically sustained and explored in parallel:

Pour briser donq', pour eteindre & guerir
Ce dur lien, ceste ardeur, ceste playe,

Je ne quier fer, liqueur ny medecine: ...      (10)

*       *       *

In the 1550 edition of *L'Olive* a dedicatory sonnet was pre-
fixed, nine sonnets were interspersed among the original fifty,
and fifty-six more were added. The interpolations are not
random; thus 23, emphasizing subjection and torment by the
lady's beauty, is placed where it can pick up from 22 the motif of
her eyes, and make less startling the transition from premature
near-ecstasy to the near-despair of the sonnet to Echo, 24. 32
finds its place next to 'Le grand flambeau ...' which also uses the
cycle of the seasons for complimentary purposes: Olive's
presence, like that of the sun in Taurus, makes May; her
absence, like the sun's departure to Capricorn, makes winter.
But 32 reworks the theme at a deeper level: spring flowers and
summer fruits perish quickly, and Olive's youthful beauty will
also fade; but autumn fruits last through winter, and the moral
and mental perfections which, though so young, she has already
acquired, will last for ever. 44, like 33, celebrates the granting of
kisses; but it is not inserted so close to 33 as to imply this to have
been frequent. In the litany which closes the first *Olive*, 46 adds
a prayer to all pitiful gods; 50 calls the universe to sympathize
with the poet, as did 54, and both 50 and 56 appeal, as did 55, to
the god of Love; and 58 forecasts the poet's death, as did 59.

The succeeding sonnets sometimes recall old themes but often
introduce others. A new start is almost made in Sonnets 60-62,
where a cluster of literary references invites help in honouring
Olive worthily. Between the first and second editions of the
*Olive* had appeared Ronsard's first four books of *Odes*, pane-
gyrical and, occasionally, erotic; but he had not yet published
his sonnets to Cassandre, *Les Amours*. He could therefore
appropriately be hailed as 'prince de noz odes' and yet invited to
turn his attention to

Le sainct honneur des nymphes Angevines.

More obscurely, 61 hints at the success of Du Bellay's own

earlier edition,

> Je voy desja le monde qui s'incline
> A la beauté des beautez immortelles,

and 62 indicates that his subject, if not his treatment, is worthy of Petrarch, Virgil and Homer, and beyond the powers of Scève and Ronsard. Compliments and appeals to Ronsard and Scève will also frame the final section of the sequence (105-106 and 114-115). There are fresh accounts, Petrarchan (63, 65) and Platonic (64), of how the poet first fell in love; new surveys of all the lady's attributes, physical, mental and moral (65-66, 69-71, 78-83, 91, 94); and perhaps a somewhat deeper and more realistic penetration of the psychology of the lover (68-70, 84-85, 92 etc.). The Petrarchan motif of the lady's veil features in 72, that of her tears in 73, that of an altar and offerings to her in 86-87. The idea of abandoning a vain pursuit is considered in 68, though rejected as impossible in 70, 76 and 92.

Pursuit in another form is the subject of Sonnet 82, where Olive is 'craintive', fleeing from her wooer into wild and inaccessible solitudes; yet she is also mysteriously identified with Diana, the virgin huntress, irresistible and untouchable, who holds her lover captive and destroys him, like Actæon, in punishment of his audacity. The unnamed 'vous ... enfans' to whom the sonnet is addressed are revealed to be not merely courtly huntsmen but all lovers, who are to take warning from the poet's fate. The rapid accumulation of detail in the first quatrain reflects the speed of the hunter's gallop; the vocatives, exclamations and interrogation convey the speaker's distress. The rhymes of the sestet reinforce the message that 'beauté' goes with 'cruauté', adventurousness with misfortune, and what grips the lover is not merely 'ardeur' but the great goddess of love herself. The calculated use of allusion, sufficiently yet not excessively obscure, hints at the incomprehensible power of the supernatural.

From Sonnet 96 onwards Du Bellay explores the theme, once more a courtly and Petrarchan one, of separation from the beloved. Here appear the motifs of jealousy, slander and bribery, so often used in mediaeval erotic poetry to menace the success of a courtly relationship and to bring out by contrast the purity of the lovers' feelings. 98 protests against the slanders of a jealous male personage of the type of the mediaeval 'losengier', the scandalmonger who interrupts so many courtly love-poems. 99 and 100 address Jealousy personified, and 101 and 102 denounce the love of gold, showing itself in the form perhaps of a rival's bribery of Olive's guardians, perhaps of the offer to her of an advantageous arranged marriage. All this apparently makes her ill (97, 103-104); although there is no evidence that she dies, as suggested by I.D. McFarlane (*28*, p.268).

The underlying Platonism of the sequence has been much increased since 1549. Sonnet 64 describes how the third component of the Platonic Trinity, the Soul of the World, lovingly imagining the possibilities of creation, formed the physical universe; similarly Olive, formed by love, sees the potential of the poet's emotions and draws and binds him to her. 74 and 79 also refer to the creation of Olive by divine influence. Meanwhile 58, 63 and 81, like the famous 113, see her as an Idea of absolute beauty in the mind of God, and the poet as enabled by love to ascend to union there with her and with Him. This Platonism, together with some velleity, in Sonnets 107-111, towards Christian repentance for his wasting time in profane love and his lack of true love for God, leads to the mystical climax of Sonnets 112 and 113. The idea, common to Christianity and Platonism, of the guided ascent of chosen souls to God, is in 112 given a more strongly Christian colouring by references to God as Providence, as Father and Son, and as Himself purifying the elect rather than insisting on self-purification as a pre-condition. With this preliminary display of orthodoxy, Du Bellay can go on to take a Christian Italian sonnet where the Platonic tinge is only faint and the objects of desire are the Supreme Good, repose and peace, and can add his own longing for 'amour', 'plaisir' and 'beauté' to make Sonnet 113 into a superb expression of pure yet passionate love for Olive.

One would not, of course, expect to find a marked development in Du Bellay's technique over a year and a half. However, he seems even more ready in 1550 than in 1549 to exploit varied rhyme-schemes; the proportion of non-Italian sestets rhyming *ccd eed* has increased markedly, but so has the proportion of sonnets with a completely masculine or feminine octave or sestet, and the proportion of sonnets (seven out of the sixty-five new ones) with feminine rhymes only. Sonnet 110, like its Italian original, is constructed exclusively on two rhyme-words, each used seven times, and Sonnet 114, though scanning perfectly, is in blank verse. The proportion of thematic borrowing from Italian has dropped somewhat in the additions of 1550, and where there is translation it is more free. With the greater variety of motifs comes, naturally, a greater variety in vocabulary and imagery, although hardly a greater one in syntax or structure.

Perhaps the most noticeable development is that most of the 1550 sonnets are richer with compressed detail and meaning than most of the 1549 ones. Sonnets 60-62 are packed with literary references, 64 and 99 with scientific, 82-83 and 89-90 with mythological, and 107-109 with Biblical ones. Sonnets such as 63 and 68-70 change their tempo and their approach not only at the ninth line, but twice or three times. The complete sequence has become a very different volume from that of 1549, which nevertheless retains a charm of its own. Critics complain of the 'absence de toute émotion amoureuse' (Weber, *32*, p.391) in both, and of any clear picture of Olive; but there is at least a discerning and imaginative portrayal of femininity, its place in the universe and its influence on a sensitive mind.

*     *     *

From richness and compression Du Bellay might have gone on to esoterism and obscurity. He is sometimes accused of having done so in his next sonnet sequence, 'Treize sonnetz de l'honneste amour', included in his *Œuvres de l'invention de l'autheur* of 1552. The charge that these sonnets imitate the *Erreurs amoureuses* of Pontus de Tyard and are *ipso facto* obscure, 'amphigourique et prétentieuse' (Chamard, *21*, I, p.250), needs to be reconsidered now that the work of Tyard is itself being reconsidered. Du Bellay does indeed share Tyard's

Platonism and Petrarchism, imitate his themes and style, and
sometimes quote him almost literally; he is playing the game of
elegant variation which he plays elsewhere with Ronsard and
Magny. What is new is his fitting into sonnet form trains of
thought much more complex than those of the *Olive*, sometimes
more complex than those of the *Erreurs* (cf. also his 'Sonnets à
la Royne de Navarre'). Punctiliously obedient to the code of
courtly love, he does not reveal whether or not the sequence is
addressed to Olive; but the first sonnet implies that it is. His
former portrait of her, Sonnet 1 explains, came from the mind
rather than the heart, owing to an incomplete understanding of
love; but Love has accepted his wish to serve Him and now
inspires him. Out of the chaos of his thoughts and feelings,
Sonnet 9 continues, Love has created order and the ability to
perceive Him; Olive's eyes are the poet's *primum mobile*.
Coveting heavenly bliss, according to Sonnet 11, by daring to
love Olive in her mortal form, the lover has become a
Prometheus tortured by her chastity. These sonnets, all
described by Chamard as 'à peu près inintelligibles', offer to the
attentive reader a constellation of images perhaps more
intellectual than emotional, but rare, tough and powerful. There
is controlled harmony in the meticulous use of *alternance* in
every sonnet, while the uninterrupted flow of the syntax reflects
the upward direction of the poet's thoughts. The use of
particularly sacred Christian imagery in Sonnet 6 (see Weber,
*32*, pp.251-52) shows especially clearly how comparisons which
may shock are intended, as often by mediaeval poets of courtly
love, not to cheapen the *signifiant* but to glorify the *signifié*.
Villey[13] said of Rabelais that he progressed from a 'jeu
d'images' to 'symboles' and then to 'idées'; perhaps the same
can be said of Du Bellay's love-sonnets.

He left his readers a final puzzle in the group of sonnets
published after his death as his 'Amours'. The overall structure
of the sequence, if it is a sequence, is not clear; and while all but
one use the *ccd eed* sestet, nine out of the twenty-nine do not
observe *alternance*. Sonnets 1-8 are concerned with how the poet
could love his lady if she would accept his service; 9-14 assert

[13] P. Villey, *Marot et Rabelais*, Paris: Champion, 1922, p.326.

that she has indeed chosen him to immortalize her and that love has mastered him, but go no further. 15-16 suddenly introduce the motif of the refused kiss, 17-20 (Du Bellay's only love-sonnets in alexandrines) that of the lady's imprisonment (or, according to Merrill,[14] her illness), and 24-29 that of the author's deafness, without any real conclusion. Merrill argued, and convinced Laumonier (*27*, X, p.50n.), that the whole is a sequence addressed to Diane de Montmorency, natural daughter of Henri II; but Saulnier (*17*, pp.111-12; *17a*, pp.121-22) points out that Sonnets 9 and 15 are chronologically incompatible, and suggests that 11 and other sonnets may be addressed to the king's sister, Marguerite de France. One may add that 17-20 may well be French renderings of Du Bellay's Latin love-poems to Faustina,[15] and that the final phrase of 22, 'la hayne en toy morte', where Merrill sees an imperfect anagram of Dyane Montmorency, makes a much better though still imperfect anagram of Antoinete Morel.[16] Saulnier (*17*, p.112; *17a*, p.122) is probably right that the so-called 'Amours of 1559' are a collection of *pièces diverses* composed at intervals during the decade; but, like the 'Treize sonnetz', most of them contain a firm train of thought, often still more compressed and intensi-fied, where mythological allusions are used with economy and force. We shall find that Du Bellay's poetry on themes other than that of love develops in similar ways.

[14] R.V. Merrill, 'Considerations on the *Amours* of J. Du Bellay', *Modern Philology*, XXXIII (1935-36), 129-38.

[15] See T. Sandre, *Du Bellay: Les Amours de Faustine*, Amiens: Malfère, 1923.

[16] Wife of Jean Morel d'Embrun, Du Bellay's patron and friend throughout the Pléiade's existence. Ronsard represents Du Bellay as 'singing' to a 'Dianette' in 1559 (Eclogue 'Du Thier', ed. Laumonier, *27*, X, p.50); but Du Bellay may have been merely paying compliments to Morel's daughter Diane.

## 4. The 'Vers lyriques' of 1549: Odes

In the same volume as the first *Olive* Du Bellay included a longer and lighter love-poem, 'L'Anterotique ['Love and Not-Love'] de la vieille et de la jeune amie'; a neat and polite epitaph on his predecessor Clément Marot; and thirteen odes, the shortest of 48 lines, the longest of 126, under the collective title of 'Vers lyriques'. It is regrettable that these odes are not republished with the *Olive* in modern editions (they are, however, to be found in *1*, III, pp.4-54); although not a part of that sequence, they were to Du Bellay an equally considerable part of what he wanted to achieve, and would have made on his public an equally striking impact, as something familiar in Latin and Greek literature but almost completely new in French. Before his journey to Italy in 1553 Du Bellay was to publish, in different collections,[17] some twenty or thirty more poems which he entitled odes or which can be classed as such, and to compose several others which he left unpublished (grouped by Chamard as 'poésies diverses', cf. *1*, V, pp.235-409); and the *Divers jeux rustiques* of 1558 will be found to include a number of 'chants' and other poems which are really his most mature odes. To neglect or fight shy of Du Bellay's odes is to neglect an important area of his work.

The ode, for Du Bellay and his fellow-poets, was a type of composition derived from classical tradition, intended to rank above the relatively simple song popular since the earliest known poetry, through his own time and to ours. A song purports above all to express emotion spontaneously flowing into the form of a lyrical outburst; reflective or meditative poetry analyses feelings, thoughts or concepts in a way usually more rational, although more or less strongly coloured by emotion.

---

[17] *Recueil de poësie*, November, 1549; *L'Olive augmentee ...* October, 1550; *Le Quatriesme Livre de l'Eneide ... Œuvres de l'invention de l'autheur*, February, 1552; *Recueil de poësie reveu et augmenté*, March, 1553.

Somewhere between the two genres, the ode sets itself to explore concepts more elaborately than a song can do, often in the form of a ceremonial address to a real person or a personification, but with a wondering admiration akin to what in religious practice is called contemplation rather than meditation. The concept contemplated, or the event which stimulates the contemplation, must be an important one of social, moral or philosophical value, worthy of attention of this sort; but friendship, love and, by way of compliment, a loved person, may be considered eligible. Following Horace, Du Bellay listed suitable subject-matter in the *Deffence* (II,4): 'les louanges des Dieux & des hommes vertueux, le discours fatal [the predestined course] des choses mondaines, la solicitude des jeunes hommes, comme l'amour, les vins libres, & toute bonne chere'.

The style in its turn must be worthy of the concept, deliberately exalted and elaborated. Du Bellay went on to say that the ode should be 'eloingné du vulgaire, enrichy & illustré de motz propres & epithetes non oysifz, orné de graves sentences [maxims], et varié de toutes manieres de couleurs & ornementz poëtiques'. Indeed, the ode may even draw attention to its own elaboration; hence, in circles like that of Du Bellay, appeals for divine inspiration or claims to have received it. The metrical structure is free: no two of Du Bellay's 'Vers lyriques' have the same metrical structure; it may be that of a simple song, but often longer lines and more complex rhyme-patterns are chosen, to reflect the seriousness of the poet's approach and the weightiness of his utterances. Like the sonnet, the ode may seem artificial; but it can provide the reader with a sense of the richness of the concept studied and of its moral and emotional importance, and leave him in a state of awed pensiveness beyond that evoked by any but the finest sonnets or songs.

\*　　\*　　\*

The first of the 1549 odes is composed in seven-syllable lines rhymed in couplets, which might at first glance seem merely a lighter variant of the octosyllabic couplets so familiar in mediaeval verse narrative and in the poems of Clément Marot.

But in every other way it would have startled the reader as did the first sonnet of the *Olive*. 'Vela brave, propre & congru commencement', complained Barthélemy Aneau,[18] seeing the exclamation 'O' and the relative 'de qui' in the first line, with the missing vocative 'Loyre' a full six lines farther on. (See Chamard, *1*, III, p.4 for Aneau's comment.) Du Bellay is, of course, aiming at prestigious impressiveness by imitating a Latin construction; but also he is imitating the irresistible flow of the river addressed, rushing the reader on through an uninterrupted sentence of twelve lines, another of four, another of eight, and so on, all full of *enjambements*. Still more, they are full of classical allusions; the aim of Du Bellay is to glorify his native province by making the Loire into a Latin river-god, and peopling the countryside with the powerful and beneficent divinities of Greece and Rome. Anjou is endowed not merely with corn and vines but by Ceres and Bacchus; its forests are alive with lascivious fauns and fugitive nymphs, the latter protected from the former by the flooding of the river, expressed through reminiscences of Horace and Virgil; its rich harvests are due to the bounty of these nymphs and of Priapus, Pales, Flora and the shepherd Apollo himself; so much so that this familiar district becomes a subject for poetry as appropriate as exotic India or fertile Arabia Felix. The ode, as becomes a hymn, begins and ends with prayer, at first for divine blessing on the province, finally (with the personal intervention traditionally permitted in the ode) for perpetuation of the fame and work of the poet himself, as his reward for devoting himself to the praise of his homeland and of a French beauty.

The 'Vers lyriques' seem to be arranged carefully to offer variety and yet suggest an implicit but logical progression of thought. Ode 3 sings the praise of Love in the same style as that of Ode 1, though in a more dancing metre; but its ebullience of delight is finally shadowed by thoughts of the coming of old age and the mortality of love, as Ode 1 is by the thought of death. Alternating with these odes come the pessimistic 2 and 4, con-

---

[18] The critic of the *Deffence* who published his comments on it under the pseudonym of Quintil Horatien; see Chamard's edition of the *Deffence* (2) which includes many of Q.H.'s comments in footnotes.

cerned with the unhappiness of man on earth; the effects of war, among them, it seems, a prevalence of suicide; the mutability of the seasons, the transience of youth and glory, the inconstancy of fate, and the impossibility of predicting the future. Ode 4, the longest of the thirteen, is dedicated to Ronsard.

It is possible, despite the scepticism of some critics,[19] that in 1549 Du Bellay was well aware of Ronsard's then unpublished odes, of which two appear to have been addressed to him before the publication of the *Olive*.[20] Odes 4 and 10 seem to be his replies, and the entire 'Vers lyriques', perhaps, his attempt to rival Ronsard's four forthcoming books of Odes. In Ode 4 he warns Ronsard against ambition for preferment and popular acclaim, wealth and astrological fortune-telling, all concerns of the courtiers; his friend is encouraged rather to seek modest lowliness and the only 'immortal' aim, the appreciation of the reading élite whom Du Bellay describes in line 108, with tongue-in-cheek satire, as 'la tourbe obscure'. Emphasis is given by adroit adaptation of Horatian borrowings: Horace's Roman pines and towers are replaced by Angevin oaks and aspens (line 100). The ideas are also driven home by rhymes which may seem facile, but are chosen and arranged in the telling *aab aab* pattern to stress a notion ('ores/encores', 4-5; 'sombre/umbre', pronounced 'ombre', 7-8; 'nue/denue', 27-30; 'nom/renom', 115-16) or a contradiction ('verdure/froidure', 33-36; 'vie/ravie', 51-54). The melancholy is intensified by the choice of night rather than day to begin and end the cycle of the hours (7-39), and of winter rather than Horace's spring to begin and end that of the seasons (19-36); and the advice to his friend is framed in hints of divine judgment (49-84 and 126).

Like the greater part of Ode 3, however, Odes 5 to 8 encourage man to seek consolation for unchangeable fate and useless anxiety in 'wine, women and song'. Ode 5, a compliment to two unidentified young girls, starts in the grand style of a

[19] H. Chamard, 'L'Invention de l'Ode et le différend de Ronsard et de Du Bellay', *Revue d'histoire littéraire de la France*, VI (1899), 21-54; M. Dassonville, *Ronsard, étude historique et littéraire*, II, Geneva: Droz, 1970, p.110.

[20] P. Laumonier, *Ronsard, poète lyrique*, Paris: Hachette, 1909, p.50.

Pindaric ode with an invocation to his lyre, that is, his own
poetic powers, and with the assertion, so frequently to be made
by Ronsard, that he can immortalize his subjects by his 'chant
qui penetre les cieux'. But the ode relaxes into a courteous
epistle, leisured and reflective, in which (as in Ode 11) the
contents of numerous typical love-sonnets are loosely strung
together with the freedom and expansiveness which the ode form
permits. We have met in the *Olive* the comparison with painting
or sculpture; the claim to operate in the sphere of eternity; the
comparison with the Graces, with the nymphs of Diana, with
dawn, flowers and jewels; the compliments to eye and voice. But
Du Bellay has space also to encourage his dedicatees with hints
of the glory of motherhood as experienced by Europa, Leda,
Danae and Alcmene. He warns them, however, that the love of
Jupiter (could he mean the love of Henri II?) may, as to Callisto,
her son Arcas, and Io, bring danger and death as well as glory.
The 'ennemy humain' of the penultimate stanza is, of course,
not the Devil but a human and humane 'enemy' in the
Petrarchan sense, a future husband, the ship that will come into
a happy harbour. No cloud obscures this final picture of lawful
marriage preferred to illicit passion.

Ode 7 praises Bacchus, in an imitation of a single Horatian
ode more faithful than is usual with Du Bellay, but dropping the
short narrative introduction to pass directly to the dramatic lyric
in which the poet represents himself as transported by mystical
Dionysian frenzy. It may be found as convincing as Ronsard's
'Chant de folie à Bacchus' of 1550, if less so than his
'Dithyrambes' of 1553 (Laumonier, *27*, II, p.177, and V, p.53).
Ode 8, like Ode 6, returns to the more typical Horatian theme of
'carpe diem'; but although 8 is ostensibly about the 'retour du
printemps', in the last three stanzas Du Bellay's melancholy
reappears, contrasting Nature's capacity for renewal with man's
finitude. This attitude culminates in Ode 9, perhaps a mere
exercise in the expression of despair on the model of the Italian
'disperata', with some influence possibly from the Penitential
Psalms. Exercise or not, it seems to be placed here to mark the
nadir of the poet's pessimism as a contemplative, as Ode 11 will
mark the lover's nadir. Demerson (*24*, p.401) finds in Ode 9

what one may also see in Ode 11, 'un sentiment de mélancolie ... cette complaisance dans les charmes de la tristesse qui en atténue l'intensité, mais en accentue la beauté'.

Again, however, Du Bellay alternates: the last stanza of Ode 8, and Odes 10 and 12, offer a different and more cheering contrast, that between the fragility of human physical and material achievements and the durability of poetry. Ode 10 returns to addressing Ronsard, not this time with slightly denigrating warnings, but with a concise summary of topics his colleague is competent to treat in poetry; discreet imitations, in well-balanced, richly-rhymed stanzas, of the styles he might adopt; and, together with some traditional self-deprecation, a glowing vision of the success he will attain. Ode 12, an epistle in all but the loftiness of its language, repeats initially the theme of universal misfortune, mutability and despair; but it sees the movement of Fortune, like that of Nature, as cyclical rather than capricious, and urges patience until time reveals truth and good fortune follows bad. The poet has learnt acceptance, and become aware of new sources of hope.

The final ode, 'De l'immortalité des poëtes', once more expresses faith in poetry. Assurance rings through it, from the initial, brusquely confident invocation of the author's Muse, whom it was not yet commonplace to treat as a sister *à la* Musset, and of Jacques Bouju, a lawyer and poet of sufficient eminence to testify to his friend's capabilities. Du Bellay chooses a strong octosyllabic quatrain whose movement into a deca-syllabic couplet, the 'vers héroïque' of the time, reflects his proposed movement (lines 5-6) into the loftiest style available to a writer. Its devices of abstraction (7-12), parallelism (7-12, 14-15, 43-44), hyperbole (20, 26, 29, 34), metonymy (8, 10, 19, 44-45), periphrasis (32, 51) and mythological allusion in general (13, 21-24, 40, 47-48) all serve to enhance the claims of disinterested-ness, true classicism and undying fame, until what would in realistic terms seem youthful presumption takes on the sonority of bardic inspiration. Above all, we find a brilliant selection and translation of classical borrowings. Du Bellay mirrors the development of Horace's Ode I,1; juxtaposes, as Ronsard was to do later, Horace's imagined metamorphosis into a swan

(II,20) and his assertion 'I shall not wholly die' (III,30); and
subtly intensifies Horace's 'separation from the populace'
(I,1,32) by the addition of a Virgilian sense of 'sainte horreur' in
the presence of divinities. In this ode, at least, Du Bellay's
pretension to equal his models justifies itself.

Some of the preceding odes, however, may be thought to be
the mere exercises of an apprentice; and all may be thought to be
little more than mosaics of borrowings from diverse classical
sources, Homer, Hesiod, Pindar, Virgil, Horace and Ovid.
These borrowings, nevertheless, are not applied as pure surface
decoration. The great classics taught Du Bellay to depict
emotions, events and relationships by means of comparison with
natural phenomena, the recurrence of the seasons, the
emergence of the sun, the flow of water or the hostility of
winter; but his real love of nature, especially that of the Anjou
countryside, leads him to adapt and vivify these images. Other
classical figures of speech, invocations and other exclamations,
imperatives and rhetorical questions, attract the reader's
attention, add interest to the rhythmic patterns and variety to
the momentum, and when repeated help to establish an inner
coherence and firmness of structure. Mythology enriches the
poetry with all the evocative power of some of the greatest myths
and deities imagined by man; we have seen Du Bellay using it in
patriotic and erotic contexts; Demerson (*24*, pp.82-86) shows
how it can also convey despair, horror, anxiety and awe, and
(p.512) can reflect the ineffable harmony between the exterior
and the interior universe.

Most of all, the influence of Horace is no superficial one; he
was evidently for the Du Bellay of the 'Vers lyriques' 'le meilleur
aucteur, dont il ... observ[ait] ... toutes les plus rares & exquises
vertuz' (*Deffence*, I,7). Even in 1549 Du Bellay had a deep
understanding of the structure of the typical Horatian ode, with
its close-packed thought which jumps from idea to idea,
connecting them apparently by mere association and often by
unexpected turns of syntax, but progressing nevertheless, with a
latent logic of its own, to a profoundly satisfying conclusion. It
is not, for instance, just that the third stanza of Du Bellay's Ode
6 quotes the first stanza of Horace's Ode I,9; irrespective of

what season is pictured at the opening, Du Bellay's sixth Ode reflects the whole movement of both Horace's fourth Ode and his ninth, from observation of nature, through gratitude to the gods and submission to Fate, on to resignation to the limitations of the human condition and enjoyment of its compensations. 'The exquisite art of rhythm and order, the clear bright speech, the quick and graceful movement of ideas, and the friendly poet who smiles at his reader'[21] — Du Bellay could not yet mirror all these aspects of Horace, but he was learning to do so. He was ready also, as we have seen in relation to his Odes 4, 7, 8 and 13, to differ with and from his source, to adapt, omit, alter and add.

\*       \*       \*

Rather than attempt to follow the general development of Du Bellay's odes through the largely encomiastic *Recueil de poësie* of November 1549 and the collections of the next four years, it will be enlightening to select from them the odes which make use of one motif, references to Ronsard. There was, of course, classical precedent for such a motif, in Horace's references for instance to Mæcenas or, still more, to Virgil. We have already noticed two odes addressed to Ronsard in the first 'Vers lyriques'; there are passing references in other odes of 1549 and 1552; and he featured prominently in Du Bellay's longest and most elaborate composition in the grand lyrical style, 'La Musagnœomachie', and in another ode in the same volume.

Although Ode 4 of the 'Vers lyriques' adopted an attitude of pessimistic warning, Ode 10, with the hyperbole characteristic of Renaissance complimentary verse, took it for granted that Ronsard was capable of the widest poetic range and destined to lasting fame. 'Gloire' for Du Bellay is nearly always literary glory; only when he writes explicitly Christian verse does it take on the meaning of moral worth. When in a 'Chant triumphal' of August 1549 he celebrates Henri II's military success and calls for suitable lyrical or epic tributes to it, he is already referring in the past historic tense to Ronsard's (yet unpublished) proof that

[21] T.R. Glover, *Horace: A Return to Allegiance*, Cambridge University Press, 1932, p.6.

he has the needed skills:

> Ronsard premier osa bien attenter
> De faire Horace en France rechanter,
> Et le Thebain (ô gloire souhaitable!)
> Qu'à grand labeur il a fait imitable.
>
>                                   (*1*, III, p.83)

References in the *Recueil de poësie* (Odes 4 and 15) to the Loir,
Ronsard's river as the Loire was Du Bellay's, imply the same
confident assumption of his friend's fame and the public's
knowledge of it. Three years later Du Bellay will neatly combine
modesty about himself with flattery of Ronsard through wishes
that he could write like his hero, in the odes 'au seigneur des
Essars' and 'au seigneur Robert de la Haye', and in that 'A
Jaques Gohory' which Chamard dates in the same year (*1*, IV,
pp.163 and 178, and V, p.253). Du Bellay modulates his tone
according to the person addressed; but whether he is composing
a panegyric on a victorious monarch, a defence of the use of
French in poetry or a compliment to a friend, the mention of
Ronsard becomes almost a shorthand symbol for the highest
achievement in poetry.

In some odes, Du Bellay extends his use of imagery until it
becomes allegory, a system of metaphors or especially personi-
fications, particularly of inward forces and feelings, which not
merely expresses meaning at separate moments but governs the
structure of long passages or whole poems. Whether with the
purpose of edifying, warning or glorifying, its effect is to make
abstractions vividly attractive or repellent in idealized or
grotesque forms, and to present their interrelations and
implications with exaggerated but memorable clarity. 'La
Musagnœomachie' of 1550, and a shorter but scarcely less
elaborate ode to Ronsard, 'Contre les envieux poëtes', published
in the same volume (see *1*, IV, pp.3 and 43), blend mythology,
allegory and real characters in idealized guise. Both move fast,
in seven-syllable lines given weight by their combination into
twelve-line stanzas.

The volume's title, 'The War of the Muses and Ignorance',

suggests the Titanomachia and the Gigantomachia, the great classical myths of the wars of the Titans and Giants against the Gods, rather than the mock-epic, then attributed to Homer and mentioned in lines 25-26, of the War of the Frogs and the Mice, the Batrachomyomachia. The latter is comic throughout, whereas Du Bellay's poem is deeply serious; but reminiscences of the Batrachomyomachia may have inspired his representation of Ignorance — by which he and Ronsard meant antiquated and unenlightened ways of thinking opposed to their own — at first by the symbols of marine monsters against which the poet sails his ship, and during the greater part of the poem by that of a chimera-like combination of ass, bear and mole. Against this horror charges Henri II, supported by his mother and sister, his statesmen and scholars, and in due course all the poets of the time, above all Ronsard. The central stanza of the 516-line poem introduces him as one of 'trois flambeaux', the others being, evidently, Baïf and, presumably, Du Bellay himself; the next stanza presents Ronsard fully, with the rhetorical question:

> Qui est celuy qui du chef
> Hurte le front des etoiles?

recalling not only the first ode of Horace but perhaps even Psalm 24 and Isaiah 63. The monster is already dying from the poets' attack when Pallas, Mercury and Apollo complete its discomfiture, although it is reinforced by Furies and three hundred Giants, whose defeat provides the climax of the poem.

'Contre les envieux poëtes' uses allegory, this time water and bird imagery, on a more intimate level, with Ronsard and Du Bellay heading their small but powerful army against the more numerous but ill-equipped and mediocre poets of the court. The 'gent noire' and the 'mille corbeaux' of stanza xvi represent their vast host, opposed by the numerically weaker but much more talented 'nouveaux Cignes'. In the next stanza, the imagery is drawn from the sport of hawking; the 'etomisseur' or saker, a trained hunting bird, representing Ronsard, has little trouble in routing the 'milan' or kite, a black bird considered untrainable for hawking. This represents the court poets, and perhaps in

particular their virtual leader, Melin de Saint-Gelais. Not only is
his name echoed, but so is one of his own poems, a 'Ballade d'un
chat et d'un milan', in which the kite Sagon attacks the sleeping
cat Marot, only to find himself captured by his enemy. Du
Bellay neatly turns Saint-Gelais's version of the Marot-Sagon
quarrel to his own use, to refer to Saint-Gelais's uncompli-
mentary recital of Ronsard's poety in May 1550; he applies
Saint-Gelais's name for Sagon to Saint-Gelais himself, increases
the irony by imitating the latter's own allegory of a battle to
portray a literary quarrel, and pushes his point home hard by the
play on names. As in 'La Musagnœomachie', the forces of
Ignorance are finally scattered, and, as in Ode 13 of the 'Vers
lyriques', the triumph of true poetry culminates in Du Bellay's
own transformation into a swan.

## 5. The Roman Sonnets:
### 'Les Antiquitez' and 'Le Songe'

So far Du Bellay has been seen primarily as the eager and earnest young student of 1549, although chapters 1 and 2 have pointed to his mature technique, and chapters 3 and 4 have shown how his love-poetry and odes developed in 1550 and later. A great break in his career, however, occurred in April 1553. During the preceding years he had been preparing and publishing new collections of poetry;[22] but he had been ill, distracted by lawsuits, to some extent losing his original inspiration, 'ne sentant plus', as he says, 'la premiere ardeur de cet enthusiasme qui me faisoit librement courir par la carriere de mes inventions',[23] to some extent perhaps waiting or searching for new inspiration. Partly out of disillusionment, 'a mes travaux cherchant quelque repos' (*Regrets*, 'A Monsieur d'Avanson'), partly impelled by 'flateuse esperance' (*Regrets*, 25), by dreams of an Italy as the latest stage of the state and culture of ancient Rome, he accepted or achieved an invitation from his father's cousin Cardinal Jean Du Bellay to accompany him on a diplomatic mission to Rome, which they reached in June. Du Bellay was to work as the Cardinal's *intendant*, household steward or secretary, and was to be still more disappointed in Rome than he had been in France.

When he returned to Paris in the autumn of 1557 he brought with him four manuscripts, all to be published early in 1558 (though some manuscript poems had been circulating already), *Le Premier Livre des antiquitez de Rome ... plus un songe ...*, *Les Regrets*, *Divers jeux rustiques*, and *Poematum libri quatuor*. Critics from Chamard (*8*) to Weber (*32*) considered that the

[22] *Le Quatriesme Livre de l'Eneide ... Œuvres de l'invention de l'autheur* (which included the 'XIII sonnetz de l'honneste amour') (1552), *Recueil de poësie* (2nd edition, 1553).

[23] *Le Quatriesme Livre de l'Eneide ...* 1552, épitre-préface 'au Seigneur J. de Morel'. See *1*, VI, p.248.

*Antiquitez* was the first volume to be composed, because of its
alternating dodecasyllabic and decasyllabic sonnets, the *Regrets*
being in alexandrines only, and because of its cryptic title of
'premier livre', never to be followed by a second. This suggested
to Chamard that Du Bellay was 'paralysé par un précoce dégoût'
(*21*, II, p.40), to Saulnier that the *Regrets* might be the intended
'second livre' (*4*, p.xxxv, and *15*, p.22), to Screech that 'premier
livre' might mean the first in French on the subject (*5*, pp.31-32),
and to Gadoffre (*10*, p.224) that a complementary treatment of
the history of France was intended. Saulnier's suggestion (which
he himself soon withdrew, *16*, p.139) seems unlikely, since the
*Regrets* appeared in January, together with the *Jeux rustiques*,
two months earlier than the *Antiquitez* and the Latin poems.
The 'second livre' of the *Antiquitez* may simply have been the
*Songe*. Meanwhile Lawton,[24] Saulnier (*15*, pp.5 and 21),
Screech (*6*, p.30) and Yvonne Bellenger (*7*, p.253) are likely to be
right in thinking that the manuscripts were composed simul-
taneously rather than successively; poems written in any mood
and in any form would be fitted into the appropriate sequence,
just as each sequence was finally to be arranged in the most
telling order.

Nevertheless, since the *Regrets* continue Du Bellay's quasi-
autobiography through and after his return to France, whereas
there is no evidence that the *Antiquitez* and *Songe* were added to
during that time, it is reasonable to postpone study of the
*Regrets* until after treating the shorter sonnet-sequences. For
accounts of the Latin poems, readers may consult Thierry
Sandre,[25] I.D. McFarlane[26] and Dorothy Coleman (*9*).

*        *        *

Considerable research on the *Antiquitez* has been done in
recent years from different points of view. The main themes of

[24] H.W. Lawton, ed., *Joachim Du Bellay, Poems*, Oxford: Basil Blackwell,
1961, pp.xviii-xix.

[25] T. Sandre, *Du Bellay: Les Amours de Faustine*, Amiens: Malfère, 1923.

[26] I.D. McFarlane, 'J. du Bellay's *Liber amorum*', *L'Esprit Créateur*, XIX, 3
(1979), 56-65.

the thirty-two sonnets are the grandeur of Rome until her over-throw brought about by *hubris*; the sovereignty of Time and Death who spare nothing; the jealousy of Destiny who wants nothing to remain eternal; the destructiveness of civil wars; variations upon commonplaces such as vanity, corruption and mutability; and the cyclic view of history. Saulnier's emphasis in *17* is on Du Bellay's 'attitude de l'historien épique' with the occasional 'couleur toute chrétienne'. For Demerson, too, Du Bellay's great interest is in 'les lois éternelles du devenir humain' (*24*, pp.326-41); for Françoise Joukovsky, 'à tous les échelons de la création des forces implacables menacent la gloire ... les *Antiquitez* sont l'histoire d'un sauvetage par la poésie' (*26*, pp.229 and 240). Griffin, still more than Saulnier, contrasts Du Bellay's Christian vision of earthly futility with his classical delight in human creativity (*12*, p.118); for Dorothy Coleman the contrast lies rather in 'an awesome respect for her [Rome's] literature and an almost sadistic delight that she has come to nought' (*9*, p.90). It is Gadoffre in *Du Bellay et le sacré* who goes furthest in his exploration of Du Bellay's 'synthèse personnelle' following a tradition of Christian humanist historical thought: 'Du Bellay cherche, au-delà de Rome ... les lignes de force de l'Histoire' (*10*, p.88). Of the succession of empires mentioned in the Book of Daniel, Rome is the fifth; is it still alive although asleep, or being superseded in its turn by a sixth? According to Gadoffre, Du Bellay rejects the candidature of the Holy Roman Empire; in the cultural domain Rome's successor will be France, in the political field there will be no successor (*Antiquitez* 6. 7-8, 16. 11-14).

As regards Du Bellay's creative methods, Demerson voices the judgment of the majority of critics: Du Bellay's inspiration is not visual or archæological (although Gray will disagree with the first finding and Gadoffre in part with the second); 'l'imagination de Du Bellay est paresseuse' (*24*, p.326). His sources, Demerson shows (like Saba and Françoise Joukovsky before him and Gadoffre and Dorothy Coleman after him), are chiefly literary; but this does not mean the near-translation, or the free composition stimulated by a translated fragment, which we saw in the *Olive*. As Saulnier comments: 'presque toujours,

là même où Du Bellay semble suivre un modèle précis, la source
est en réalité multiple' (*16*, p.133). Dorothy Coleman shows how
materials from Roman history and literature and from
mediaeval Latin combine to form for Du Bellay a 'paysage
intérieur' (*9*, p.94), Griffin how he uses the techniques and
devices of traditional rhetoric. Gray paradoxically claims that
Du Bellay's 'exercice poétique' is to convey 'le néant' by means
of 'langage qui se voudra effacé … vocabulaire réduit …
abstractions … images usées … économie de moyens … la rime
… esclave … au thème' (*11*, p.43), but even he goes on to study
more positive devices. Saulnier's *cours de Sorbonne* (*15*) is still
the critical work which ranges most widely among the techniques
of the *Antiquitez* as among their ideas, while his article (*16*)
penetrates deeply into their deliberately difficult style. Saulnier,
Demerson and Gadoffre unite in showing how the great mytho-
logical figures of the Giants, Pandora, Jason and Romulus
symbolize humanity with its besetting sins, subject to the
ineluctable judgment and sentence of historical and moral
causality.

Several critics note the apparent lack of order or development
in the content of the *Antiquitez*, although for Françoise
Joukovsky this may be deliberate on the part of this 'poète de
l'ambigüité': the disorder of the poems would mirror that of the
ruins. The sonnets, however, as ruins may, seem to show some
grouping into clusters. The dedicatory sonnet to the king and the
first two sonnets of the sequence are all positive and optimistic
panegyrics: behind them is the idea of the *translatio* of the
domination of the world by monarchical government and
artistic achievement, its transfer from Rome to France by the
providential movement of history. Such a legacy, a glory for
those who have left it (Sonnet 1, lines 3-4), is also a glory, pride
(Au Roy, 7) and happiness (*ib.*, 9) for those to whom it is left;
and Du Bellay's own sequence, inspired in general by Rome and
at many points by Latin literature, forms a sample of the legacy
and a happy omen (Au Roy, 7-8, 13-14). The Romans, though
dust (1, 1) and in 'enfer' (1, 6; not the Christian hell but the
classical Hades), are still 'divins', immortalized by their own
literature (1, 1-4); it is armed with the power of their own rites

that Du Bellay invokes them (see Saulnier, *15*, p.40, and Demerson, *24*, p.339). Sonnet 2, with the help of abstractions, adjectives derived from proper names, and future tenses, neatly packs into the octave and the succeeding couplet an enumeration of the traditional Seven Wonders of the ancient world, among which Rome was not included; the simple dignity of the last line emphasizes 'Rome's catholicity and calm assurance' (Griffin, *12*, p.128). The optimistic tone is sustained through all three sonnets by the choice of detail, choice and recurrence of expressions (*beau(x)/belle, divins, gloire, grand(eur), hault(e)(s), (bien)heur(eux), loz, saincte*) and final cadences: 'bienheureux presage', 'gloire plus belle', 'miracles du monde'.

It is with Sonnet 3 that the 'deploration' of the *Antiquitez* title begins (though it should be noted that Cotgrave (*23*) defines 'deplorer' as 'bewaile, moane, bemoane, lament for', without the pejorative overtones of the modern 'deplorable'). The note of lamentation is struck insistently in this sonnet, as in the neo-Latin epigram which is its source, by the repetitions and repeated contrasts shown by Griffin (*12*, p.125) and Dorothy Coleman (*9*, pp.102-05). But the note of condemnation already makes itself heard, if not in 'orgueil', which can be admiring, at least in line 7 (where 'pour donter' can mean either 'in order to subdue' or 'because of having subdued', and 'quelquefois' can mean 'once, at last') and in line 10; Du Bellay's first charge against Rome is not her conquests but her civil strife. In Sonnet 4, however, it becomes clear that the reference to 'orgueil' is indeed a condemnation, if not of Rome's empire-building, certainly of her *hubris*, 'wanton violence arising from the pride of strength'.[27] The sonnet is again a fairly close translation of a neo-Latin source, but finally a sadistic caricature in relation to the original and to the map of Rome; in the Latin, the Cœlian and Esquiline hills pin down the feet, the Aventine and Viminal the hands of the buried Titan; in Du Bellay's rendering the figure of the fallen giantess is impossibly contorted. Saulnier dismisses the suggestion that the poet was merely constrained by metrical considerations; yet it is true that he could have written

[27] Anon., *A Lexicon abridged from Liddell & Scott's Greek-English Lexicon*, Oxford, 1903.

'le dextre pied' in line 12, but not 'sur une main' in 14; he may have solved the problem by reversing the two terms with a grim smile at the result. Sonnet 5 repeats the substance of 1, but uses the approach of 4; Du Bellay invokes now no 'divine spirits' but Rome identified only by all that remains of her, her 'morte peinture'. No glorious soul will come at his summons, only a horribly automated corpse; and if Roman literature still perpetuates Roman fame, it is merely as an 'idole', 'a shape, image, spectre, phantom ... a fancy ... an idol, false god'.[28]

However, Sonnets 6 to 9 return to the tone of admiration shaded less with criticism than with melancholy regret. 6 (on which see especially Griffin, *12*, pp.134-36, and Dorothy Coleman, *9*, pp.105-08) is inspired by four lines of *AEneid* VI and by the 'tradition de l'allusion encomiastique à une fécondité bénéfique pour la nation' (Demerson, *24*, p.331). Rome is portrayed as Cybele, the Phrygian Earth Mother, according to Virgil grandmother of a hundred gods, who wears a mural crown and rides in a chariot drawn by lions. Rome had produced more great men than the fifty sons of Priam of Troy; her power extended to the limits of the earth, her daring braved heaven; only Romans could destroy her, as in the Civil Wars to which line 10 seems specifically to refer by quoting Horace's reference to them (*Epode* XVI, 2). Only Time could destroy Rome, retorts Sonnet 7, whose last Petrarchist tercet, or rather that of its Italian source, is criticised by Screech (*5*, p.280) as irrelevant; but Marchi (*13*, p.160) defends it on the ground that Rome herself can play for her admirers the role of a beloved woman, while H.G. Hall[29] sees the tercet, still more its source, as hinting at the sequential triumphs of love, of chastity over love, of death over chastity, and finally of resurrection and eternity. Sonnet 9, brilliantly elucidated by Saulnier (*16*, pp.127-29), goes on to take Rome's destruction by Time as proof of the eventual annihilation, not merely of the earth and all sublunary things, but of the universe itself. The structure of this sonnet relates it

---

[28] *Ib.*, *s.v.* εἴδωλον

[29] H.G. Hall, 'Castiglione's *Superbi Colli* in relation to Raphael, Petrarch, Du Bellay ...', *Kentucky Romance Quarterly*, XXI (1974), 159-81.

closely to Sonnet 7; the rhythm of the first line of each is almost identical, and the eighth line of each provides a climax in relation to which the last line, for all its implications, is aurally an anticlimax.

The difficult Sonnet 8 forms a slight interruption; perhaps its alexandrine metre necessitated its placing between 7 and 9 instead of after the latter; Time, it will end by saying, has brought Rome down, but not entirely. It starts from a Latin epigram by the Scottish humanist Buchanan, who had been teaching in Paris during Du Bellay's time there. Lines 2-4 of the French render line 2 of the Latin a little clumsily; the city's only limits, Du Bellay is trying to say, were those of the terrestrial world. Buchanan's remaining two couplets contrast the celestial and infernal worlds which still remained to be conquered: the piety of the early Popes won heaven, their 'good' posterity ran at full speed to hell. Du Bellay's comment is more ambiguous: 'vertu(eux)' and 'brave' may or may not be ironic; line 8 may mean 'measured the distance from earth to heaven' (but literally, 'from heaven to earth', with more possible irony in another allusion to the fall of the Titans) or 'measured heaven by the standards of earth'. However, the sestet reasserts the greatness of Rome with less ambiguity; it turns on the legend that a human skull, unearthed at the laying of the foundations of the temple of Jupiter on what was to be the Capitoline Hill, gave the latter its name, being taken as symbolizing Rome's future headship of the world. Although states are destroyed by time, comments Du Bellay, Rome has not fallen so low as to invalidate the prophecy.

Sonnets 10 to 13 meditate on the paradoxes to which the unequalled greatness of Rome gave rise. It alone could put an end to itself, its own progeny (10) alone could destroy it. It could be destroyed only by a power (11) which itself came to nothing; no one, not even Jupiter (lines 13-14), can boast of having destroyed Rome, since the instruments of destruction, the barbarians, were themselves later destroyed. Rome in defeat (12) is still superior to the rest of the world (13). The impression of superhuman grandeur is conveyed by a massed battery of artistic devices. There is myth: Rome produced more soldiers than

Jason, unconquerable by any Hercules (10); the barbarians were
new children of Mars, new Giants or Titans (11, 12); the figures
of Cadmus and Cain, Jupiter and Tiber (13), loom in the back-
ground. There is hyperbole: Rome's armies (10. 8) filled the two
houses of the Sun, explained by Saulnier (*16*, p.119) as earth and
sea or earth and sky, but perhaps heaven and the underworld to
which the sun passes with every sunset, the abodes of the deified
and of the other dead. There are conventional metaphors (10. 6,
etc.), abstractions (11. 2-8, etc.) and periphrases (10. 1-2, etc.),
heavy with the weight of tradition, vividly recreated in Du
Bellay's imagination, and strengthened by elevated and forceful
vocabulary. One sonnet (11) is constructed from only two
sentences, the other three from a single sentence each. Antithesis
is particularly apt for the expression of the theme of the
*Antiquitez*; in 11 and 12, quatrain and tercet are matched
against quatrain and tercet, producing an interrupted antithesis;
Sonnet 10 exploits the more familiar opposition between octave
and sestet, and 13 an almost Shakespearian one between the first
twelve lines and the last two.

If wonder at 'la grandeur ... qu'ilz ... ont laissé[e]' pre-
dominates in Sonnets 10-13, what predominates in 14-16 is pity
for its reduction to the 'rien qu'ilz ont laissé', symbolized by the
thrice recurring adjective 'poudreux' (-euses, -euse). Sonnet 14,
accumulating images from classical sources, ends with a double
paradox: 'les vaincus' must be the subject of 'osent', 'les
vainqueurs' the object of 'desdaigner'; but are 'les vaincus' the
barbarians, so long dominated by Rome and seen at the moment
of their revenge on her? Are they the Romans, quietly superior
even in their 'poudreux tombeaux'? 15, finely appreciated by
Dorothy Coleman (*9*, pp.109-11), renews the conjuration of
Sonnet 1, by the potent reminder of the earliest Romans' con-
struction of 'cest orgueilleux sejour', reinforced by a prayer
(since 'n'enferment' is a subjunctive) for their liberation from
imprisonment by the nine loops of the infernal river Styx. The
invocation becomes more intimate with the suggestion that at
least one old ghost may still be present among the 'reliques
cendreuses', and, after the crescendo of line 11, falls to the anti-
climax of the last tercet and the closing cadence.

16, placed at the midpoint of the whole sequence, is a master-piece of technical as of thematic structure. Each quatrain follows an identical pattern: comparison introduced by 'comme', second element of image introduced by 'puis' and completed by infinitives at the beginning of lines 4 and 8. The symmetry of the predetermined rhyme-scheme of the octave is complemented by parallel grammatical constructions, past participles used adjectivally in lines 1 and 8, verbally in 4 and 5. The first of each pair of *b* rhymes, present participles, is also closely related to the following line, 'ondoyant' introducing 'mille flotz', 'tournoyant' introducing 'une aile plus large'. The build-up of force evoked in each quatrain is aptly brought to a sudden halt in lines 4 and 8. Although the third image has only a tercet in which to be developed, the pattern is repeated: com-parison, present participle, infinitive. A new rhythm is intro-duced, but also a certain new unity, by insistence upon selected consonants, principally *s*; perhaps this echoes the noise of the octave's waves and wind no less than the hissing of fire. At the caesura in line 11 the series of images gives place to the subjects of the comparisons. Skilful use of *enjambement* creates a displaced alexandrine:

>             ... ainsi parmy le monde
> Erra la Monarchie ...

After this unexpected yet totally acceptable rhythmic change, Du Bellay returns to his original imagery, only for the reader to discover that the sonnet has been constructed in *vers rapportés* (cf. p.25 above). Instead of developing the series of images line by line or phrase by phrase as is usual, Du Bellay has expanded the sequence so that only one image features in each quatrain and the first tercet, and has compressed it into six syllables in line 13 to force it finally on one's attention. The 'dying fall' of line 14 epitomizes the fact that 'entropy constantly threatens the natural world' (Griffin, *12*, p.132); 'destruction and evanescence are conveyed to the reader' (McFarlane, *28*, p.275) through sense, imagery, pattern and sound.

Sonnets 17 and 18 continue the historical approach of 16, but are packed with allusions which demand commentary before the structure can be grasped. 17 borrows from Horace (and perhaps, according to Vianey, *31*, p.195, Guidiccioni) the opening vision of the circling eagle, symbol of Divine watchfulness for human error and readiness to punish it. So long as the forces of Rome devoted themselves to serving and maintaining the Divine order, the latter was not menaced by the Giants, who here represent not the Romans but the barbarians. But the growing presumptuousness of the Romans, soaring to a height which left earth too far below, had to be punished by God's permitting the barbarians to break the peace and destroy Rome. The present Holy Roman Empire is only a fancy-dress worn by the German descendants of the barbarians, who are raising modern Rome to a position which they believe will equal its ancient one, while they remain blind to the Divine vengeance which may again destroy it. The self-repetition of history is mirrored in the cyclic construction of the sonnet itself, the last line almost repeating the first two, and is still more clear in the succeeding sonnet, 18. The crescendo of power and presumption reappears, the primitive peasants of the Roman *campagna* making themselves into a royal house, increasingly greater power being acquired by the two consuls elected for twelve months, the one dictator for six, the Emperor for life. Du Bellay sees the Popes, with their claim to be shepherds and servants of the people, as an anticlimax whose weakness and inefficiency come by another Divine punishment. The contrast is delayed until near the end of the sonnet and underlined by the rhyme-scheme: the rhyming couplet of lines 9-10 is linked by sense and syntax to the preceding quatrains, and thus accentuates the distinction between them and the final four lines.

Sonnets 19 to 22 are built each on a single simile, in 20 that of the swelling and bursting storm-cloud, in 21 that of the navigator shipwrecked at the end of his voyage; the references to Thetis, the misty sea-nymph of *Iliad* I, 359, and to Hannibal as the war-god of Libya, are merely decorative. 19 follows in more detail the myth of Pandora, the bride given by Zeus to Epimetheus, whose wedding-gift was a jar containing plagues according to Hesiod, blessings according to later writers, both for Du Bellay.

When Pandora opened it, the blessings flew back to heaven, the plagues were left on earth, hidden 'jusq'icy', says the poet, with another satirical reference to the modern Rome of the Popes. The octave lists indiscriminately all the things which Rome once held under her control; a sharp 'Mais' introduces the contrasting sestet, with its creation of order out of chaos and its clear separation between good and evil. 22 takes up the theory of Pythagorean science, that it is after 36,000 years that the cycle of the stars' motions and of history will be completed and the constituent elements of the universe will return to their original arrangement. Although the four sonnets all turn on comparisons, these are placed with wide variety: the image occupies the octave of 20, the sestet of 22; in 21 it manifests itself gradually from line 5, in 19 becomes suddenly explicit in line 8. All four sonnets, however, have a 'dying fall', a final line leaving a picture of ruin, annihilation, wreck and chaos.

Sonnets 23 and 24 are perhaps the only two where the note of admiration for Rome is completely lacking, save in 23's opening commonplace. An exceptional Roman, the younger Scipio, apparently went against the whole political and military tradition of his nation in advising mercy to the Carthaginians, their hereditary enemies; he recommended this, Plutarch and Du Bellay suggest, only so that a continuing external threat might keep the Roman people from presumption and internal strife. Civil war, the dominant theme of both sonnets, is traced to its sources. 23 does this in moral and psychological terms: idleness leads to discontent, pride, envy and ambition, which in turn lead to disharmony and breaking of peace, as between Caesar and Pompey. 24 sees civil war from metaphysical and theological viewpoints: as Horace (*Epode* VII) pointed out, it is unnatural to animals; it must be occasioned by destiny or Divine punishment, for ancestral or original sin, perhaps Romulus's manslaughter of his brother Remus; but Saulnier (*16*, p.120) comments on 'la discrétion dont use le poète ... il laisse facilement ... l'imagination osciller de l'aventure de Remus et Romulus à celle de Caïn et Abel'. Each sonnet conveys its complex train of thought by smoothly flowing clauses adroitly shaped into quatrains or tercets, till 24 ends in an absolute participial construction where, still more vividly than in the second tercet of 23, a moment of history stands out as typifying and explaining all that was to ensue. Du Bellay's choice of grammatical flexions to supply rhymes, *-ir*, *-ieux*, *-ez*, *-elle* and *-ment*, and of conventional abstractions, periphrases and images, makes the task of expression easier; but the very fact that these images and abstractions come from long-standing tradition 'confère à l'évocation un prestige et un retentissement' (Saulnier, *ib.*), makes them arouse echoes in the subconscious mind.

With an abrupt change of tone, Du Bellay groups next five sonnets which form only what his title calls 'une generale description' of the 'antiquitez de Rome', but which come nearer than the other twenty-seven to pictorial images of Rome's splendour at its height, as mirrored in its architecture and sculpture and with the help of its literature. 29 presents the city as a microcosm, 25 as a community's self-expression which can never be imitated materially but which a poet might hope to reflect in words, 27 as an architectural triumph which papal patronage of the arts is recreating on the model of the old. The alexandrine sonnets are more subtle: 28, at first glance a simple picture, is in fact largely a translation from Lucan (*Pharsalia*, I, 136-43), and so a use of Rome's own resources to achieve her own self-portrait; 26, with the help of Horace and perhaps also Ovid and the Bible (Zechariah 2 and Revelation 21, as suggested by Griffin, *12*, p.129), uses the idea of the microcosm with more imaginative depth than 29: a true picture of Rome would have to extend to the limits of the world. These five sonnets rely chiefly on enumeration, giving an impression of overwhelming abundance of spectacular detail; echo-effects, most obviously in the sestet of 26 and the last two lines of 29; allusion, sometimes direct, sometimes conveyed through periphrases (like the references to Orpheus and Amphion in 25 and that to the Giants in 27, line 2), sometimes merely echoing a phrase or passage from an ancient poet; and, in every sonnet, an epigrammatic or paradoxical close, strong and haunting.

The last three sonnets of the sequence decline into a deliberate anticlimax which reflects the fate of Rome herself. They still recall in scattered lines her greatness, her beauty and the master-pieces of her literature, Virgil being quoted in 30 (though Griffin, *12*, p.134, prefers Mark 4, 26-29), Lucan[30] in 31. But these glories have been levelled out, by the fighting of the civil wars and the destructions of the barbarian invasions, into 'une vague campaigne', fields of stubble and rubble. The sixteenth-century meaning of 'vague' was not so much 'formless, obscure' (*New English Dictionary*) as 'void, empty; waste, idle' (Cotgrave, *23*, who adds that it could mean — as in Italian — 'faire, beautifull, cleere, bright'). Du Bellay recognizes the charm of even the ruins of Rome, crystallized in the picture of the serene and luxuriant cornfield; this charm, the concluding Sonnet 32 indicates, is what he has tried to convey throughout the sequence. But nothing earthly can achieve immortality; Rome fell, his own verses will be forgotten; all he will be able to claim is that he was a humble, 'bas' pioneer in commemorating in French the 'peuple à longue robbe', the 'gentem togatam', as Virgil himself had described them (*AEneid*, I, 282). The sonnet and the sequence end with a simple, almost prosaic phrase, but one which, like so many of Du Bellay's, picks out and leaves lingering in the mind a detail which suggests more than it says.

\*     \*     \*

The *Antiquitez* and the *Songe* both have the ruins of Rome as their central image, but the treatment of them is quite different in each collection, and recent research has suggested that the *Songe* is more than a lamentation on the passing of time or on Rome's present state of decay compared to her former magnificence. Gadoffre (*10*) has argued convincingly that it is an anti-Papal (more strictly a Gallican) pamphlet, condemning the immoral excesses of Julius III and Paul IV, their nepotistic choice of cardinals and some of their policies. Whilst earlier research by Chamard (*21*, II, p.45), Saulnier (*15* and *16*) and Demerson (*24*, pp.326-41) identified literary sources, Gadoffre's

---

[30] See especially F.M. Chambers, 'Lucan and the *Antiquitez de Rome*', *Publications of the Modern Language Association of America*, LX (1945), 937-48.

commentary has clarified many of the more obscure allusions to contemporary realities: Sonnet 2 describes the Tempietto of S. Pietro in Montorio, 3 the Vatican obelisk, 4 the Arch of Janus Quadrifrons. In 5 the oak of the Capitol has split into the Holy Roman Empire and the Papacy, and the owl of 7's line 13 balances the crow of *Antiquitez* 17. Du Bellay is taking the opportunity to issue a firm warning, occasionally audible also in the *Antiquitez*, that, because of the conduct of various successors to St Peter, Rome is in danger of disintegrating yet again.

The basic structure of the *Songe* is adapted from Petrarch's Canzone 24 to Laura; but perhaps, as in 'Contre les Petrarquistes', Du Bellay felt that in the Italian song some moving images, assembled in a promising structure, had been wasted in the praise of a single human being, however perfect. Skilfully he replaced the lament for Laura's death by eloquent evocations of Rome's rise and fall. Additional visions and details, together with borrowings from classical and biblical sources, enabled him to expand six twelve-line stanzas and the three-line coda into fifteen sonnets. But the importance and success of the *Songe* do not lie merely in adaptation of sources. One of the great attractions of these sonnets, as of the *Antiquitez*, is the way in which different levels of interpretation and appreciation present themselves to the reader. Moreover, critics, especially Gadoffre and Demerson,[31] have revealed different ways in which the thematic content, external architecture and expressive devices of the *Songe* give it strong outward and inward unity.

The dream-setting of the *Songe* is made very clear. The opening lines of the first sonnet set the scene and allow the poet to develop his dream-sequence, uninterrupted till the final line of Sonnet 15, when he is abruptly awakened. Because dreams are often mysterious or unintelligible, the reader is more tolerant of the obscure allusions and strange scenes evoked. Where the *Antiquitez* suggested a slow and lengthy process of decay, here

---

[31] See also D. Russell, 'Du Bellay's emblematic vision of Rome', *Yale French Studies*, XLVII (1972), 98-109; and Margaret B. Wells, 'Du Bellay's sonnet sequence *Songe*', *French Studies*, XXVI (1972), 1-8, from which the next paragraphs are adapted.

the destruction of Rome is sudden, rapid and total. A very tight structure replaces the vague, free-flowing sequence of ideas in the *Antiquitez*; one disaster follows another immediately and vividly. Despite the dream-setting, the detailed descriptions of the ruins seen are much more precise than in the *Antiquitez*, and in the *Songe* Du Bellay remains consistently accurate in his description of natural phenomena. Yet into these sonnets he has further woven a series of allusions and carefully chosen epithets which appeal to the reader's subconscious rather than to his conscious mind.

Deeply impressed with the mutability of material things and the instability of human institutions, Du Bellay draws his imagery from the two life-giving and life-destroying elements fire and water, one (if not both) of which appears in every sonnet of the sequence. Seven of the sonnets symbolize Rome by the river Tiber, evocative of fertility and life; the mounting and radiant flame of Sonnet 11 also suggests the ideas of birth and growth. But still more, throughout the sequence, fire and water symbolize ruin and death; they are responsible for the collapse of Rome, either as direct agents (7, 11, 13 and 15) or by close association with other forces of destruction (2, 3, 4, 10 and 14). Where it is not directly related to the downfall of Rome, the elemental image is retained in the entire setting of a dream-episode (1, 5, 8, 9 and 12). Only in Sonnet 6 are fire and water not immediately obvious, but even there liquid is evoked in words such as 'allaictant', 'soif', 'estancher' and 'sanglotz'. The selection of imagery within the elemental framework is fully consistent with sudden destruction — 'tremblement', 'tempeste', 'foudre', 'orage impetueux' and so on. This imagery, greatly strengthening the unity of the sonnet-sequence, shows that the dream-setting does not preclude careful and tight control of the apparently chaotic presentation.

Both the creative and destructive powers of fire are illustrated in the very complex Sonnet 7, which also assumes familiarity with the sixteenth-century view of the world in the form of a chain of being which incorporated every aspect of creation. The fiery 'Soleil', ruler of the heavens, symbolizes the height of glory and power aspired to by the eagle, king of the birds, replacing the Petrarchan phoenix as a personification of Rome. The idea of supremacy is maintained in line 8; the 'lieu ou des Dieux est le temple', with the sun, represents the source of inspiration for the eagle's flight, and is thus symbolic of life or *raison d'être*, rather than of death. However, the sun's property as destroyer of life is also apparent. The eagle, flying too close to the sun, is burnt in a 'tourbillon de feu' and reduced to earth, the lowest of the elements. Out of the ashes is born a worm, one of the lowest creatures in the animal world, which will develop into an owl (or perhaps, according to Demerson, *24*, p.335, a crow), symbolizing not wisdom but the seeking of 'darkness rather than light' (John 3,19). A cyclic effect is thus created; the sun is responsible for life and death in a recurring pattern.

Perhaps Du Bellay was first attracted to his Petrarchan source by the emphasis on sudden change in the series of phrases, 'in poco tempo', 'repente', 'breve ora', 'poco spazio', 'subito' and 'in un punto'. The *Songe* goes beyond the Canzone, however, in attention to detail. Destruction by fire is always the result of a flash of lightning, not of a slowly burning conflagration; water, however violent or tempestuous, is used to typify a long, slow process of destruction. The structure of the sonnet lends itself to an unexpected ending: in the sestet, in the final tercet, or even in the last line the tone of the poem changes, the ideas are reversed, a course of events is interrupted, terminated or summed up by an epigram. In the *Songe*, words such as 'soudain' stress this poetic device yet more. Poetic and thematic structures parallel one another to a high degree.

\*       \*       \*

Both in the *Songe* and in the *Antiquitez* (until 31), Du Bellay alternates regularly decasyllabic and alexandrine sonnets. This can hardly have been because he was unsure of the suitability of the longer line or doubted its acceptability (despite its reputation as prosaic; see chapter 2). More probably the variation of line-lengths was deliberate. Adages taken from or modelled on those of Erasmus fit equally well into either:

Rome de Rome est le seul monument,
Et Rome Rome a vaincu seulement.     (*Antiquitez* 3)

Rome seule pouvoit à Rome ressembler,
Rome seule pouvoit Rome faire trembler

(*Antiquitez* 6)

The alexandrine permits neat antithetical or chiasmatic constructions:

Les foibles fondemens de la grande Cité.

(*Songe* 14)

Rome fut tout le monde, et tout le monde est Rome.

(*Antiquitez* 26)

Yet two decasyllables can be used in a less compact, but still tightly controlled antithetical sequence:

Ce qui est ferme, est par le temps destruit,
Et ce qui fuit, au temps fait resistance.

(*Antiquitez* 3)

Rome vivant fut l'ornement du monde,
Et morte elle est du monde le tombeau.

(*Antiquitez* 29)

When the effect of the alexandrine is lengthened by a series of *enjambements*, as in *Antiquitez* 18 and 20, a feeling of inevitability is created, so that the final lines have strong impact; but the same effect, although more often rushing to a deliberate anticlimax, can also be seen in the decasyllabic sonnets of the *Songe* (5, 7, 9, 11). Du Bellay also shows how both alexandrine and decasyllable can accommodate polysyllabic proper names and adjectives derived from them (*Antiquitez* 2, 4, 6 and 31, but also 25, 29 and *Songe* 5), creating majestic resonance not only by their mythological and symbolic value but also by their very sound.

It is probably in the *Antiquitez* and the *Songe* that Du Bellay makes use of the widest range of poetic techniques. Borrowings, quotations and allusions invite cross-reference from sonnet to sonnet and to their sources; the unforgettable phrases in which Roman poets expressed themselves are part of their civilization and its most durable legacy. Repetition, apostrophe and antithesis impart intense force. Petrarchan stylistic devices are remarkably prominent, despite the total difference of matter: opening phrases such as 'Qui voudra voir', 'Telle que' and 'Non autrement que' (*Antiquitez* 5, 6 and 20), the construction of *Antiquitez* 13 upon the repeated negative comparison introduced by 'Ny', and, of course, the whole development of the *Songe*. Even the vocabulary, as in *Antiquitez* 7 and 13 and *Songe* 12 and 13, comes from Petrarchan love-laments. By reminding the reader of traditional love-sonnets, Du Bellay highlights his ability to create new possibilities within a well-established form.

## 6. The Roman Sonnets: 'Les Regrets'

The *Regrets* present a different view of Rome — its con-
temporary appearance, inhabitants and way of life — portrayed
almost, it seems at first glance, by a different author, simple,
personal and spontaneous. However, this sonnet-sequence
should be seen primarily as literary creation, and not relied upon
as accurate autobiography or photographic self-portraiture. Du
Bellay has composed for himself a complex *persona*, a dramatic
character, his own and not his own, in which he presents himself
as if masked and costumed for public performance. Now he is
the poet in the act of creation, now the exile lamenting his
beloved France, now the harassed official in the Cardinal's
household, now the ironic observer of the Papal court, now the
returned traveller who finds his homeland not up to expectation,
and finally the half-reluctant court poet. This *persona* has been
formed from many sources, beginning with the Ovid of the
*Tristia* with 'the hopes and wishful dreams, the pains and
shuddering fears, the fretting and lonesome musing, and the ebb
and flow of his pride'.[32] Critics[33] unite in explaining how Du
Bellay's fusion of the Ovidian tradition with that of Roman
satire accounts for the changes in tone in the sequence, chiefly at
Sonnet 53, but at other points too.

The apparently spontaneous and colloquial style, advertised
by the author as a rejection of convention (Sonnet 4, lines 9-10),
is itself part of the ironic convention. It was normal in Latin;
had been prevalent for a century in Italy, in a tradition of satiric

[32] H. Fränkel, *Ovid*, University of California Press, 1969, p.117.

[33] See Yvonne Bellenger (*7*), Dorothy Coleman (*9*), Gray (*11*), Griffin (*12*) and
perhaps especially L. Wierenga, '*Les Regrets* de Du Bellay. Satire et Elégie? A
propos de l'édition M.A. Screech des *Regrets*', *Neophilologus*, LVII (1973),
144-55.

sonnet-writing well known to Du Bellay;[34] and in France was already the style of Marot and his disciples. Du Bellay has the subtlety and concealed richness of Marot, with a wider gamut of insights, evocations and harmonies, and with the powerful weapon of the alexandrine sonnet form, providing more range than the *dixain* and more impact than the *épître*. The air of simple naturalness can mislead; because any reader who has suffered disillusionment can often identify himself with the 'je' of the poems, he is led to consider them as essentially a record of Du Bellay's own feelings; but even the poet's claim that he is writing about what touches him most deeply must be treated with caution, for it is part of his explanation for his venturing into this style of writing, new for him.

One must read each sonnet of the *Regrets* with an eye for quotation or parody, reference or implication, mockery or self-mockery. As in the *Antiquitez*, literary borrowing, mythological allusion, and traditional themes such as that of Fortune are present, though insinuated concisely and discreetly; they extend the sonnets into a further dimension, distancing the topical observations and hinting at the universal validity of the judgments. One must listen too, for plays on words or on sounds, changes of rhythm which indicate changes of tone, and unexpected emphases. In the end, far from being soothed by simplicity, we may find ourselves lost among Du Bellay's multiple levels of irony.

Although the tight thematic and structural unity noted in the other two Roman sonnet-sequences is not obvious here, the *Regrets* are not assembled haphazardly. There is a progression, though in places implicit and associative rather than logical; thematic changes are supported by tone-changes and verbal devices; the elegiac tone is reserved for those sonnets which suggest the poet's exile, physical and spiritual; the most satirical outbursts are reserved for the Papal court. This reinforces Gadoffre's suggestion (*10*, pp.181-82) that the *Songe* and, to a lesser extent, the *Antiquitez* are essentially anti-Papal pamph-

---

[34] See Vianey (*19*), pp.71ff. and Yvonne Hoggan-Niord, 'L'Inspiration burlesque dans les *Regrets*', *Bibliothèque d'Humanisme et Renaissance*, XLII (1980), 361-85.

lets; the *Regrets* is one too, although much more besides.

One more unifying factor in the sequence is the continuing influence of Petrarch. His style is reflected not only in the elegiac sonnets but also in the satiric ones, if with a touch of parody; Du Bellay poses as a Petrarchist lover lamenting in turn his own banishment and his lady's infidelity. Petrarchan sonnet-structures based on repetition and antithesis, such as 'Ceulx qui ... Moy qui ...' of Sonnet 5, are even more suited to satire than to simple regret. The very title of the volume, though more obviously indebted to Ovid's *Tristia* than to Petrarch's *Rime*, recalls also, at least to Screech (*5*, p.13), the catchword of the latter, 'sospiri' (*Rime* I, i, 2; I, cxx, 1; *Trionfi* I, 1, etc.).

\*     \*     \*

Du Bellay's partial self-identification with Ovid is made clear in the dedication 'A Monsieur d'Avanson' and the sonnet 'A son livre', which stem respectively, in a manner that would have been evident to every contemporary reader, from the openings of Books IV and I of Ovid's *Tristia*. However, the poems may certainly be called original, and not only for the reason given by Chamard, 'parce que l'accent est sincère' (*1*, II, p.45); both are adapted and finally developed independently to fit the poet's own circumstances. The Dedication, Screech points out, seems to have been conceived in Italy and rehandled in France, since the past tenses of the first two stanzas are inconsistent with the present tenses later; Screech's edition summarizes the alterations and additions to line 72, where Du Bellay breaks away from Ovid, and Lapp[35] indicates the enhancement of these by sound-effects and the 'bold telescoping' of the myth of the Muses and that of the Sirens. The style of the original passages (5-6, 31-40, 73 *et seq.*) matches perfectly that of the translated passages and of Ovid himself, with the evaluation of poetry as at once the fruit and the solace of grief (74-80: *Trist.* III, i, 9-10); the abstinence from self-judgment (85-88: I, vii, 12, 'qualia-cumque'); the compliments to an influential friend (89-104: I, v;

---

[35] J.C. Lapp, 'Mythological imagery in Du Bellay', *Studies in Philology*, LXI (1964), 109-27.

I, ix, etc.); and the claim to immortality (108: III, vii, 50-52).
Besides 'A son livre', other sonnets soon following contain
Ovidian echoes: 1(9-10) recalls *Tristia* IV, i, 91:

Ipse mihi — quid enim faciam? — scriboque legoque,

not used in the Dedication; Ovid is directly recalled in Sonnet 10,
indirectly in 36; and the comparison of the poet with Ulysses
goes back to the *Tristia* (I, v, 57-58; III, xi, 61-62).

'A son livre', after its first quatrain, moves into the Horatian
style of satire, 'a variety of themes treated in a personal way,
irony and wit written in a lower style than the Odes, moulded
into a *ryme en prose* with *ordo* and *compositio* still the
prominent features' (Coleman, *9*, p.75). Sonnets 1 to 23
establish that Du Bellay's choice of this style is conscious and
deliberate. They are largely negative in language; the author
specifically rejects various poetic styles, the philosophic gravity
of Ronsard's recent *Hymnes* (1), the supernatural inspiration of
Hesiod (2) or of Ronsard's *Odes* (3), and the graceful beauty of
the love-poetry of Horace, Petrarch and Ronsard (4), in favour
of (ostensibly) simple colloquialism. Saba (*14*, p.180) sees the
persistent negatives as a lament for lost inspiration, Bellenger (*7*,
p.80) as a regretful renunciation of 'haute poésie', Gray (*11*) as a
negation of an entire approach to poetry (p.62), if not of poetry
itself (p.14): 'il tend vers une poésie qui serait savante par et dans
son dépouillement' (p.63). It is certainly 'savante'.

Sonnet 5, for example, although called 'facile' by Vianey (*19*,
p.113), 'monotone' by Weber (*32*, p.423) and 'simply bad' by
Dorothy Coleman (*9*, p.75), is packed with exquisitely econo-
mical insinuations.[36] Love traditionally makes a poet of the
lover; but line 1 hints that lovers have nothing better to do than
to write poetry. Line 2 raises the question whether 'honneur' and
'gloire' are the same, and whether either is real; 3-4, whether
those who are 'pres du Roy' are to be distinguished from mere
'courtisans' or identified with them. The surprise second half of
line 5 suggests that arts specialists are mere *poseurs* and pedants;

[36] See also C.E. Nelson, 'Enumeration and irony in the *Regrets* of Du Bellay',
*French Review*, XXXVI (1962-63), 268-70.

6 brings out more clearly the idea of posing, and questions the reality of virtue. 7 puts drinkers and writers of drinking-songs on the same level as all those previously featured; 'fables' in 8 was the Renaissance term for poetic fictions, which might or might not contain profound truths. 9-10 indicate that scandal-mongering is not the best way of amusing. The motif of boasting, already glimpsed in 1-2 and apparent in 4 and 6, comes to a climax in 11-12, making one ask whether the supreme flatterers of 13 are self-flatterers. 14, appearing to continue the formal structure but in tone and meaning contrasting sharply with all the preceding lines, puts forward one of Du Bellay's deceptively simple and straightforward personal statements, leaving one wondering how far the poet's 'malheur' lies in his familiarity with all those he has pilloried.

A deeper note is struck in Sonnets 6 and 9, on which every critic of Du Bellay comments; and its overtones are heard in 7-8, where Marguerite de France and Henri II are complimented with no irony, in 16-17 and in 19-20. In Sonnet 8 it is not Petrarchan structural devices, but the over-familiar vocabulary of the Petrarchan lover that takes on new dimensions. The single sentences which fill up each quatrain and tercet suggest sustained feeling; but the rhyme-words hint that all is not as it seems. The poet's letter of love is addressed not to Olive but to Ronsard, 'la moitié de mon ame'; the well-worn Horatian phrase recalls the myth of the Androgyne, and emphasizes the exile's separation from his friend in the idyllic France of his imagination. Of the stock group of erotic rhymes *ame/enflamme/dame/flamme*, only 'dame' retains its conventional meaning; 'l'ardeur qui l'Italie enflamme' is no longer love or love-poetry which excites, but intrigues and conspiracies which infuriate. The unflattering rhyme *rien/Italien*, especially when contrasted with the positive *mien/bien*, underlines the author's dislike of Italy. On the other hand, the purely Petrarchan line 5 has as its real function to introduce the next line, with its implication that the inspiration derived from the king by the subject-poet equals that derived by the lover-poet from his lady. The repetition of 'sainct(e)' and 'cela', and the parallelism of the possessives 'ta', 'ton' and 'mien', leave no doubt as to Du

Bellay's intention. 'Soleil' is expanded in meaning to become not only Henri II but France herself; it is in her that the sun of favour produces the vines of poetic inspiration, frozen and withered by the wintry moral climate of Italy, which the enumeration of line 14 reduces to a single perception. A final ironic touch is added by the disguise of the Italians as the Hyperboreans, legendary worshippers of Apollo who lived in perpetual sun, but in fact inhabitants of the farthest North, in unending winter.

In Sonnets 24 to 38 the poet's voyage to Rome becomes the main theme. The personal touch is achieved here, as in the opening section, by the predominant use of 'je' and 'me', Petrarchan enough, but also by more twisting of Petrarchan tradition, Sonnet 24 picking up Petrarch's motifs of 'regret' and 'repentir', and Sonnet 25 his celebration (*Rime*, Sonnet 39) of the moment when he first fell in love. Whilst the journey evoked is ostensibly a sea-voyage with its attendant perils, a parallel is clearly drawn with Du Bellay's literary adventure into the uncharted waters of his new style of writing. The irony of the opening of the famous Sonnet 31 is sometimes missed. Although Ulysses became the hero of the Odyssey and Jason won the Golden Fleece, the voyage of neither was a happy one; Jason's was attended by treachery, subterfuge and murder; Ulysses' was a ten-year struggle to return home despite storm, shipwreck, imprisonment and the loss of all his men. Neither enjoyed a happy home-coming; Ulysses had to use violence to rid his home of self-invited guests; Jason found his father murdered by the latter's half-brother. And neither lived out his life in peace among his family; Jason's wife murdered her children, and, by some accounts, Jason killed himself; Ulysses was sent on further wanderings and, according to some, killed by his illegitimate son. 'Beau' can be ironic as in Sonnet 32; the poet dreams of a happiness which his prototypes did not achieve.[37]

Du Bellay's fine sense of rhythm is demonstrated in this section, where he develops the description of his uncertainty, doubts and disappointment by repeating, echoing or reversing

[37] Cf. G.H. Tucker, 'Ulysses and Jason: a problem of allusion in sonnet XXXI of the *Regrets*', *French Studies*, XXXVI (1982), 385-95.

terms and constructions. In Sonnet 33, for example, he portrays inner torment by repeating the verbs and the key-words 'si' and 'longue'; by self-interruption and self-contradiction (line 11); by pairing questions which expect opposite answers (9-10); and by a line 13 which almost exactly repeats line 1 in reverse order, and brings the poet back to his original position. However, varied rhythmic patterns reflecting his inner conflict are produced by the interruption of line 1 by 'si tu l'entends'; the *enjambement* of 5-6, not repeated in 7-8; and the crystallization in the single line 11 of contrasts expressed in two or more lines before. The Latin proverb echoed in the last line neatly sums up the poet's whole uncertain frame of mind.

The elegiac tone of this section is replaced by ironic bitterness and declared indignation in Sonnets 39-49, where Du Bellay describes his official duties in Rome. Because of the contrast between 'être' and 'paraître', the temperament he claims to be truly his and the manner he is forced to assume, it is only natural for him to make great use of antithesis, as in Sonnet 39; but he also obtains effects from rhetorical questions and accumulative conditions introduced by 'si'. The contrast between himself and Ulysses, which appears with gradually increasing clarity from the Dedication to Sonnet 31, is now sharply pointed in Sonnet 40. Perhaps to vary the tone and show himself capable of genuine affection, Du Bellay devotes Sonnet 49 to his uncle the Cardinal; four sonnets to the latter's gentleman-in-waiting Vineus, who ranked high above a mere secretary but was evidently ready to treat him with friendliness; and Sonnet 41 to a friend recently dead. Chamard (*1*, II, p.84) and Eugénie Droz (*3*, p.62) identify him with Jacques Tahureau, a minor follower of the Pléiade; but nothing suggests that their relations were as close as the sonnet implies. It might be another young writer of the time, Jean de La Péruse; a patron of the Pléiade, Jean Brinon, mourned by Ronsard in the *Continuation des Amours*, 'Verson ces roses ...'; or an unknown friend in Anjou or Rome.

Sonnets 50-76, addressed to various friends, relatives, patrons and enemies in France and Italy, amplify the portrait of the exiled poet. To cope with his situation he adopts philosophical attitudes — stoical in 51-52, mildly epicurean in 53-55, empirical in 56. The difficulty of 55, addressed to the unidentified but evidently legal-minded Montigné, lies in its use of technical terms, familiar enough, as Screech says (*5*, p.124), at the time. With the help of Cotgrave's dictionary, it may be translated as follows, the legal terms being italicized: 'Montigné (for you are experienced in lawsuits), if one of those gods who have *higher jurisdiction* promised us *undisputed possession* of all our goods, *pledging us* by Styx his whole godhead *as security*, he has ill *performed his promise* to us, and we ought to *contest the case* before Jupiter. But if one cannot *oppose* the Fates, who *pronounce sentence* according to the *decrees* of Destiny, we shall make no *appeal*, *seeing that* we are no more *exempt from jurisdiction* than the rest of mankind, who have like us *lost their action at law*. Yet if Trouble wished to *distrain on* our freedom of mind, by the forcible means of calamity, we would *protest against* the *carrying out of the seizure*.' Du Bellay, as in the Dedication (line 60), ranks 'fantaisie' higher than do others of his time, who define it as mere opinion; for him it is Sonnet 38's 'libre affection', over which nothing unworthy can 'tyrannise'.

The author soon finds other consolation in depicting his companions and his relationships with them. Sonnet 60's friendly dig at Ronsard's *Hymnes*, some dozen of which are mentioned by name and contrasted with one of his own *Divers jeux rustiques*, is by no means the only one in the *Regrets*. Sonnets 1-4, as has been seen, parody and reject his style among others, and the teasing of 23 risks being hurtful; but any parody of Ronsard in 16-17 and 19-20 is milder, and there is no malice in references such as those of 8-10, 26 and 72. Sonnets 63-73 make less friendly comments on victims whose anonymity Du Bellay preserves, although critics have made guesses. His discretion is in keeping with the traditions of Horatian satire, described in the *Deffence* (II, 4), and to which Sonnet 62 pays tribute and affirms allegiance: it is also a prudent move for anyone criticising powerful public figures. Sonnet 76, slyly pointing out how both writers and readers enjoy satire more than eulogy, forms the transition to the important watershed of 77.

\*        \*        \*

Sonnet 77 introduces the central and most caustic section of the *Regrets*, the portrayal of Rome. Ambiguously, Du Bellay declares both that he is not here writing of ancient Rome and its religion, as in the *Antiquitez*, and also that he is presenting only the manifest and well-known failings of the Papal court. He admits to using the approach of comedy; one must relax sometimes. But it is not that he is deliberately aiming to veil his protests; they are genuine, and his laughter is merely the involuntary grimace, mirrored by repeated *i*-sounds, of a man poisoned by the plant *sardonion*. Du Bellay works in Sonnets 77-127 on three different scales. Many single sonnets provide miniature surveys of the city or the court; 80 evokes four dissimilar scenes; 81 glimpses different moments in the election of a Pope. But many sonnets are further grouped into clusters, one revealing different facets of the Papal court, another picturing the city's 'courtisanes'. Finally, all the fifty-one sonnets will be found to add up to a total picture of life in Rome.

The first and most general sub-section (78-86) opens mildly, for Sonnet 78 admits the presence of good, and in 79 the accumulation, anaphora and antithesis of lines 1-10 can be seen as an elegiac complaint about the poet's condition. But both enumerations are deceptive, leading the reader down unexpected paths. Lines 11-13 of 79, identical in structure with their predecessors, turn to open satire, while line 14 reveals its irony only on re-reading. 78, listing seven Italian states only to dismiss them with the double-edged compliment of line 4, shifts to the assertion that the triple crown, the heraldic device of the Vatican, symbolizes three vices, driving the point home by the rhyme of 'feintise' with 'eglise'. The sestet (like the sonnets to follow) hints at far more vices than three, increasing in line 14 not merely, as might have been expected, to the seven deadly sins, but to all the evils of the world. The technique of enumeration, traditional, according to Yvonne Hoggan-Niord (*art. cit.* (note 34), p.379), in the burlesque description of towns, continues in the selective tour of Rome formed by Sonnets 82-86, and is supported by a brilliant choice of detail. For instance, 82's picture of Rome in general is found to be much more precise after study of 83's picture of Rome in war-time.

82's line 10 is counterbalanced by 83's line 4, the liberty and idleness of 82's last tercet become the debauchery and unemployment of 83's first tercet, and the rumours of 82's lines 9 and 14 swell to those of 83's last line.

Sonnets 84-86 show one of Du Bellay's greatest strengths: his exact observation and telling satire of the behaviour of courtiers. Enumeration reflects their varied duties (84, 7-10; 85, 1-2; 86, 1-3 and 9-11); more rapid enumeration mirrors their more hectic activities (84, 5-6 and 12-13), which become more and more disreputable. Du Bellay does not deny that he is himself made one of such courtiers by his place in the Cardinal's suite; but the careful line to be trodden between appropriate and inappropriate resemblances to them is shown by 85's complex mingling of positive and negative infinitives. Unexpected juxtapositions ('flatter un crediteur ... courtiser un banquier ... seigneuriser chascun'), italianisms (86, 4-6) and stinging rhyme-words ('huis/Juifz', 'compte/honte') drive home Du Bellay's points, as does the final summary, 'Voila ...', extending over one line in 84, two in 85, three in 86. Play on word-sounds pervades the last tercet of Sonnet 86 and acts as an introduction to the next sonnet-cluster.

The conflict of attraction and repulsion aroused by the courtesans, the 'Nymphes Latines' of Sonnet 90, is reflected in the choice of allusions in Sonnets 87-90, 93, 95, 99 and 100. Alcina, modelled on Homer's Circe, an infernal Venus, both siren and harpy, was the wicked enchantress of Ariosto's *Orlando furioso*, who subjugated Ruggiero and transformed the English knight Astolpho into a myrtle. They were saved by Melissa with her magic ring, as Ulysses was by Mercury with a magic herb, and brought safely to the realm of Queen Logistilla, who presided over pure and true love, as did the celestial Venus of Sonnet 93. With these stories the goddess Fortune invoked in 96, Pyrrha of 99, who re-created women after the Flood, and Hannibal of 95 have no connection; but mention of them maintains the classical atmosphere, the feeling that the poet is in the power of antique forces, and the idea that modern Italians are unworthy of their ancestors and the ancient names they bear, with which Sonnet 100 terminates the sub-section.

In this sonnet, and in those just preceding, colloquialisms of Du Bellay's own time are introduced, in jarring contrast: the 'martel' of 92, 'peler' of 93-95 and 'bufle' of 95 and 96, respectively denoting jealousy, venereal disease and bankruptcy. Sonnet 91 stands out among its fellows. It is a threefold parody: of ideal beauty, negated point by point in the imaginary subject described; of that subject, mercilessly caricatured; and of the style of her supposed Petrarchist admirer, struggling to adapt his vocabulary to her unusual 'beautez'. Du Bellay's model is a sonnet by the Italian burlesque poet Berni, who was in his turn, as Marchi (*13*, p.225) points out, parodying a serious sonnet by Bembo; but Du Bellay has altered Berni's order to return to the conventional mediaeval progression from the head downwards, goes considerably further than Berni in that direction, and makes a final *pointe* independent of Berni. Nelson (*art. cit.* (note 36), pp.271-73) shows that the sonnet is less static than it seems, moving from standard idealization ('as we finish line 4 we are still not certain that we are reading a parody') to grotesque realism, and thence to a moral judgment ironically expressed. But even quatrain 1 begins to reveal the intention of parody, imitating Berni's incongruous pairing of adjective and noun: line 2's 'crespe' and 'doree' are the traditional adjectives for the beloved's hair, and line 3 similarly misplaces 'crystal' and 'grand'. Parody is also evident in the monotony of the exclamatory structure, and the perfunctory rhyming of past participles, diminutives and infinitives. Sonnet 92, by contrast, is remarkable for the straightforward detail of its description, even though line 1, as Griffin remarks (*12*, p.143), is a malicious echo of one of Ronsard's sonnets to Cassandre. The rhyme-words, 'frizer', 'choisie' and 'deguiser', stress effort on the part of the *courtisanes*; 'moisie' evokes not only their flesh but their whole way of life. Sonnets 97 and 98 do not feature prostitutes, but the victims of an outbreak of religious hysteria in 1554-55,[38] supposedly countered by exorcism. Perhaps these two sonnets are placed here to hint at a transition to Sonnet 101, without making the juxtaposition too blatant.

[38] See M. Viatte, 'Du Bellay et les démoniaques', *Revue d'histoire littéraire de la France*, LI (1951), 456-60.

In the satires on the Papal court (101-126) Du Bellay makes little use of ironical praise; he has no wish to be taken for a friend of the Papacy, and in Gallican France there was no danger in being known as a foe to it. The sonnets, however, attain brevity, sting and weight through a rich assortment of other rhetorical and allusive devices. Enumeration is used again in 101 and many others. Eight start from or end with a proverb or a commonplace. 103, 104, 108 and 109 imitate an elegy, an epitaph or a speech ascribed to a statue. Virgilian tags are echoed in 114, 115 and 116, and commonplaces of classical science in 117 and 125. 110 uses the *vers rapportés* of the *Olive* (see above p.25), and 113 puns on names, then believed to have occult or providential significance: it would not be mere chance if the sound or meaning of a person's name indicated something of his character or destiny. The surnames of the last three Popes had been del Monte, Cervini and Caraffa. Du Bellay makes the *cerf* into a *biche*, perhaps merely to scan, perhaps to hint at Marcellus II's virginal life and delicate health.

The sonnets of this cluster move away from the tradition that satire should be generally applicable; 108 claims in lines 5-6 the right to pillory individuals by name, and ends with a precise attack on a cardinal identified by Screech (*5*, p.182) and Marchi (*13*, p.253). Popes Julius III and Paul IV are censured as personally unworthy of their office; they are criticised for their past records (102, 105), their gluttony (104, 106), their nepotism and homosexuality (103, 105, 106, 113), their aspirations to secular power and splendour (106, 107) and their involvement in politics and war (110-116, 124); and their cardinals and officials are blamed for imitating them (101, 102, 105, 107, 112-115, 118, 119). Except for hints in 117, on the universal tendency to spiritual degeneration, no reference is made to the Popes' religious or pastoral duties, and Du Bellay's neglect of this topic implies theirs (the criticism becomes explicit in the *Ample Discours au Roy* of late 1559 (*1*, VI, p.191), lines 503-14). Sonnets 114 onwards move to more general reflections: 114 and 116 picture Rome on the verge of war with the Emperor Charles V; by 122 hostilities have begun, and 123-126 feature the truce of 1556.

Sonnet 127, one more enumeration, is Du Bellay's farewell to Italy. Balance and antithesis appear not only in line 1, but in the contrast of line 2 with it. It becomes clear that lines 4 and 5 equal line 3 in their implications and force when it is remembered that by Church law not only murder but also usury and the adultery or fornication which led to bastardy were sins. Line 6 is the most damning of all the octave; in the light of Christian fideism, merely human reasoning had little weight as a basis for faith. The frank simplicity of line 7 reflects the attitude it portrays, and leads to the further antithesis of line 8, 'You may imagine the rest', says Du Bellay cryptically, hinting both at what follows 'volupté' — the mind goes back to 'bastardise' — and at other sins which may accompany it. 'Si' ('however') interrupts the line, as the author remembers a lawsuit in France which is going badly for him; France is more notorious than Italy for bribery of judges and other unscrupulous use of power or influence. But this is not such a compliment to Italy as is suggested by Vianey (*19*, p.106), Gadoffre (*10*, p.55) and Bellenger (*7*, p.107); the first quatrain of the sonnet implies that Italians are satisfied with other means of attaining their ends, and the 'quelque' and 'du tout' of lines 10 and 11 are not wholly eulogistic.

This sonnet is followed by two, and the octave of a third, which move into a major key of triumph and delight unprecedented in the *Regrets*. Du Bellay pictures his homeward voyage, north along the coast of Italy (the Tyrrhenian Sea), still beset with the storms, reefs and darkness which Rome has meant for him; but he looks forward to the open sea of the Western Mediterranean, where a French sea-god and his attendant minor gods and nymphs will bring him safe to shore, calming the waves and shutting in the sea-monsters. In an unnamed French harbour he sees himself welcomed by past and future patrons and friends. The Erasmian tag 'patriae fumus', which formed a hemistich of Sonnet 31, also provides one for 130, and the soft *m*, *s* and *ou*-sounds of its first quatrain reflect the sweetness of homecoming. A final quick look back at Italy sees nothing worse than distant 'vice', Circes and Sirens, while the poet can claim a loyalty to his standards which merits reward. Suddenly the harmony is broken by the same thought which interrupted

Sonnet 127, and the author vows either to return to Rome or to open a new satiric sequence.

*       *       *

At first glance the sonnets immediately following 130 are puzzling. Sonnet 131, it seems, might have been placed anywhere between 77 and 127; Sonnets 132 to 138 record a journey by land from Rome to Paris, incompatible with the imagined journey by sea of 128-130. From 130's relation to Latin poems exchanged between Dorat and Du Bellay, Vianey (*19*, p.107), deduces that it was composed soon after the author's return to France; perhaps for a moment he intended it not merely as the close of a section, but even as the close of the *Regrets*. 131 is also a relatively late sonnet; the reference in lines 2-3 dates it in March 1557 at the earliest; it could well have been written six months later. It may be that Sonnets 131 onwards are really a second volume of *Regrets*, a new series of satiric complaints which crystallized in Du Bellay's mind during the months between August 1557 and January 1558, and into which he fitted the recent Sonnet 131 and the vivid jottings from his travel-diary, 132 to 138.[39]

The first hundred and thirty sonnets are often seen as the best part of the *Regrets*; but one need not think of the last third as either anticlimax or irrelevance. Du Bellay found as much to 'regret' and satirize in France as in Italy; any illusions about his homeland dissolved as quickly as his earlier illusions. His reception was lukewarm; Ronsard, for example, perhaps piqued by his friend's banter, wrote no welcoming verse; and opposition to the Pléiade still flourished. In the court of Henri II, as in the French law-courts, Du Bellay found as much corruption as he had unearthed at Rome. Worse, this time, his own integrity as a poet was threatened (Sonnet 144).

His comments on poetry and poets have to be viewed in the light of what he said elsewhere on these topics — in the

[39] Cf. Screech, *5*, p.205: 'Nous suggérerions de considérer les soixante sonnets suivants comme les *autres œuvres* que nous promet le titre original des *Regrets*'. On Sonnets 134-136 see A. François, *Les Sonnets suisses de Du Bellay*, Lausanne: Librairie de l'Université, F. Rouge, 1946.

*Deffence*, in his prefaces, and in a lengthy satire composed in his last years, 'Le Poete courtisan'. Only thus can one appreciate the irony underlying the apparently serious advice to aspiring court poets. The presence of an introductory 'si' in Sonnets 139, 140 and 154, and in line 4 of 145, makes the irony obvious; but it is less so in 141 and 142, where there is doubt even whether 'Amy' and 'Cousin' are common nouns or proper names, and where the author permits some lines to be taken at face value:

Ne commets ton secret à la foy d'un chacun,   (142, 5)

In 143, 144 and 146 irony is discarded in favour of a frank examination of the difficult role of the satirist.

147, 149, 153 and 155-158 celebrate the power of the written word. The first two contrast it, not with crumbling edifices and monuments, but with the spoken word, and in particular the cheap witticisms and jibes of the courtiers and court poetasters. While the author finds amusement in these, and in their crude attempts at flattery and imitation (149 lines 12-14, 150), he is indignant when his own verses are subjected to mockery (150 lines 12-14, 151). But to his friends, the true poets of the Pléiade, he offers reassurance in such genuine compliments as 147, 148, 155 (despite its rueful sestet) and 156. 147 and 152 incidentally offer Ronsard, if not an apology, at least an adjustment of differences; Ronsard's poetry, and his own, will find whatever fame they deserve. 156 is a brilliant imitation, in a mere fourteen lines, of the simplicity of the first two poets complimented and of the highly individual styles of the last three.

Much of the skill in Sonnets 139-156, and their interest for us, lie in the constantly changing tone and the kaleidoscopic effect of the delicate variations of touch. One must approach each sonnet separately, uninfluenced by one's impressions of its neighbours. The wide-ranging style includes pastiche, parody and allusion; imagery drawn from Erasmian adages and from everyday life; climactic *pointes* and epigrams; and subtle manipulations of blocks of lines. Many of these sonnets, like the Roman ones, start with enumeration, but by the sestet or the last tercet modulate into generalization, detached comment or logical conclusion; and two show a chiasmatic structure, the last line of 139 forming a mirror-image of the first, the last line of 140 reversing the thirteenth.

The transition from the praise of poetry and true poets to the praise of individual members of the court of Henri II is formed by the cryptic Sonnets 157 and 158, which few critics have studied in detail. They form a nominal compliment to Clagny, the architect of the Louvre; but one cannot take seriously 158's final claim that they are mainly concerned with him. They describe a work which Du Bellay is composing (157, line 7) or is going to compose (158, line 1). It will be a homage to the King, as is shown by the prominence given to his love (158, line 4) for Diane de Poitiers (lines 7-8); still more, a tribute to the Muses, the forces who preside over the arts and inspire artists; above all, according to Gadoffre (*10*, pp.224-25), a tribute to the French monarchy and its achievements throughout history. 'Il est placé sous le signe des muses grecque, latine, florentine et française; des quatre ordres architecturaux, attique, dorique, corinthien et ionique (*R.* 157); et des quatre poètes majeurs: Homère, Virgile, Pétrarque, Ronsard (*R.* 158) ... grille de symboles à correspondances ... vision de l'Histoire ... revendication de la primauté culturelle française au nom de la *translatio studii*.' Gadoffre does not explain in what sense Homer shows 'Attique ... naifveté' (157, 10-11), but Castor has already done so (*20*, pp.77-81); it is the spontaneous, inspired ability to be 'true to Nature in all senses of the word'.

But also, Gadoffre does not explain why Du Bellay should see modern Italy, and not ancient Rome or mediaeval France, as the 'corps d'hostel' (157, line 14), the main block of his proposed palace. Is he admitting, in a moment of insight, that there is more Italian influence on his own work than Greek, Latin or French? Is he characterizing, not a work he has still to write, but the works he is about to publish? One might select the *Antiquitez* as reflecting Virgilian gravity, *Regrets* 1-130 as using Petrarchan artifice, *Regrets* 131-191 as complimenting French notables in a fashion led by Ronsard; though if the *Divers jeux rustiques* are Greek in their 'naifveté', they are hardly Homeric. At least it seems that the last two lines of 157 hint that the

*Regrets*'s portrait of Italy, elaborate in its satire of luxurious free-living like that for which antique Corinth was notorious, is a substantial and important part of his work to date.

Whatever Du Bellay may have envisaged as his 'palais magnifique', he now proceeds to portray the court of Henri II in sonnets of compliment. They may remind the reader of those to Ronsard and Scève in the *Olive*, or the nine odes among the 'Vers lyriques' which were dedicated to named individuals; but their content is more crisply realistic than that of the earlier sonnets, and their applicability to their dedicatees is more pointed than that of most of the odes. They should not be dismissed as mere flattery of people in high places. Certainly, like Ronsard and most poets of his time, Du Bellay needed to gain and keep the favour of patrons in the court and the Church, the only way then of making poetry pay. But admiring (if sometimes discreetly critical) attitudes to his betters were an integral part of his outlook on life; their actions affected his, their achievements thrilled his royalist patriotism; and his deep sense, like Ronsard's, of the role and power of poetry made it natural for him to put his feelings into verse.

Sonnets 159-191 are arranged in a carefully devised series or pattern of portraits, such as so often decorated a Renaissance ceiling or wall, although there is no evidence of mathematical exactitude. Fifteen are to different people of rank or note, headed by Diane de Poitiers; only Jean d'Avanson, to whom the *Regrets* as a whole are dedicated, enjoys three sonnets, one shared with Cardinal Bertrand. There follow seventeen in praise of Marguerite de France, Duchess of Berry, the king's sister and the kind and practical patroness of the Pléiade since 1549. Of these, 174-176 and 190 focus on her alone; the intervening sonnets, more unusually, compliment her indirectly through meditations or compliments addressed to other patrons or friends, many of whom have already been the recipients of sonnets portraying Rome. Thus the approach of the earlier *Regrets* is continued (as the theme of return is in 174); pure praise is set off by contrast with the earlier irony or satire; and a process of climax, as in 181, 186 and 189, ranks Marguerite above all other dedicatees or subjects of verse. The last sonnet of the volume, as in duty bound, praises the king.

The style and structure of these sonnets are suited to the courtly and eulogistic tone. Structural balance is carefully achieved, as in Sonnet 170 whose symmetry is obvious, or in 165, built around a 'moins ... plus ... plus' gradation, and given further inner coherence by repeated use of positive future statements. The lengthy sentences often fill an entire quatrain or tercet, suggesting the stately, measured tread appropriate to court ceremonies. Points are made by the use of abstractions, superlatives, and references to the hierarchy of the classical gods or to the Great Chain of Being. The allusions are less esoteric than those of Sonnets 147 or 156; but straightforward praise sometimes has a sting in its tail, as in 163. The ending of 168 in particular is ambiguous, subjecting the Cardinal of Lorraine to

Le libre jugement de la posterité.[40]

It is doubtful, however, whether the ending of 191 is what Screech (5, p.191) calls 'un bon éclat de rire'. As in Sonnets 164 and 178, Du Bellay is aiming to show respect and humility; his play on theological commonplaces is calculated at most to elicit a quickly suppressed smile at his irreverent ingenuity.

In the *Regrets*, Du Bellay shatters previous conceptions about appropriate content for the sonnet, and that with a startling variety of approach. His tone ranges from elegiac to satirical, embracing all intermediate nuances; he incorporates a rich assortment of technical devices, without letting one dominate; he varies his sentence-lengths to suit the poem's mood; he exploits to the full the structural possibilities of the alexandrine, and the different line-groupings available within the sonnet form. It is impossible to point to any one sonnet as being typical or representative of the *Regrets*.

[40] See M. Smith, *Joachim du Bellay's Veiled Victim*, Geneva: Droz, 1974, pp.25-26; but also Gadoffre (*10*), p.73.

## 7. The 'Divers jeux rustiques'

Some critics find the lightest collection of 1558, the *Divers jeux rustiques*, hard to judge or to value highly. For Chamard it is 'très inégale' (*21*, II, p.211), for Dorothy Coleman 'a patchy collection' (*9*, p.74). Gadoffre and Gray neglect it; for Saulnier, 'ce recueil n'est qu'un beau sourire' (*4*, p.lxiii); and indeed Du Bellay himself had offered it as merely 'un entre-mez delectable' (dedication 'A Monsieur Duthier', line 38). However, its contents can to a great extent be seen as the pursuit to a higher or deeper level, and sometimes to a culmination, of trains of thought and exercises in style which we have seen throughout his development. We have studied sonnets which were in part or in origin translations; closer translations explicitly offered as such appear among the *Jeux*. We have seen his treatment of love and use of satire; both appear in the *Jeux*, in a freer and more roomy form than that of the sonnet. Many of the *Jeux*, indeed, are unpretentious odes; and many are far richer in subtly concealed art than they may seem at first glance.

The title has been traced to various antecedents: *jeux* suggest 'trifles' like the *Nugae* of Nicolas Bourbon (*Nugarum libri octo*, Lyons, 1538), 'rustiques' recalls the Latin use of 'silva' to mean a miscellany, like Ambrogini Poliziano's *Silvæ* of 1492. The closest parallel is doubtless the *Lusus*, in some editions *Lusus pastorales*, of Andrea Navagero himself, which inspired Du Bellay's 'Vœux'. It has not yet been suggested that at the same time Du Bellay might be recalling with some precision Rabelais's description of Gargantua's monthly holiday:

> Ponocrates, pour le sejourner de ceste vehemente intention des esperitz, advisoit une foys le moys quelque jour bien clair et serain, auquel bougeoient au matin de la ville, et alloient ou à Gentily, ... ou à Sainct Clou. Et là passoient toute la journée à faire la plus grande chère dont

ilz se pouvoient adviser, raillans, gaudissans, beuvans d'aultant, jouans, chantans, dansans, se voytrans en quelque beau pré, denichans des passereaulx, prenans des cailles, peschans aux grenoilles et escrevisses. Mais, encores que icelle journée feust passée sans livres et lectures, poinct elle n'estoit passée sans proffit, car en beau pré ilz recoloient par cueur quelques plaisans vers de l'*Agriculture* de Virgile, de Hesiode, du *Rusticque* de Politian, descripvoient quelques plaisans epigrammes en latin, puis les mettoient par rondeaux et ballades en langue françoyse. (*Gargantua*, chap. 24, ed. Lefranc.)

The *Regrets*, still more the *Antiquitez*, would indeed have been the product of a 'vehemente intention des esperitz'; in the *Jeux*, Du Bellay transposes the *Moretum* and Navagero's 'Votæ' into a French countryside very like that of Gentilly and Saint-Cloud. His satirical badinage parallels Gargantua's 'raillerie' and epigrams, his translations the classical quotations and bilingual compositions, his love-poetry Gargantua's bird-catching — 'dénicher des cailles' could then mean to find success, especially with girls,[41] for whom 'passerelle' was a term of endearment. His 'Villanelle' approaches the ballade form. Whether or not the title of the *Jeux rustiques* precisely echoes Rabelais's 'jouans' and his references to Poliziano's 'Rusticus' (one of the *Silvæ*) and Cato's *De Re rustica*, Du Bellay is certainly remembering similar real excursions, of which Ronsard describes one in 'Les Bacchanales ou le folastrissime voyage d'Hercueil' of 1552 (cf. Laumonier, *27*, III, pp.184-217). The combination of boyish relaxation with cultured conversation and literary exercises came naturally to Renaissance scholars, and is happily reflected in the make-up and tone of the *Divers jeux rustiques*.[42]

[41] Huguet (*25*), *s.v. caille*, 1, first quotation, and 3, last quotation.

[42] The preface, describing 'les … heures … que j'ay employees à la composition: c'est le temps qu'on donne ordinairement au jeu, aux spectacles, aux banquetz, et autres telles voluptez …' also seems to echo Rabelais's *Prologue* to the *Gargantua*: 'à la composition de ce livre seigneurial, je ne perdiz ne emploiay oncques plus ny aultre temps que celluy qui estoit estably à prendre ma refection corporelle …'

Broadly the poems may be divided into three groups: the poems numbered 1-13 and 15 by Chamard[43] are translations; 14, 16-26, 33 and 37 are love-songs or meditations on love;[44] 27-32, 34-36 and 38 are satires or jokes. But many poems come under more than one heading; there are translations which are love-poems, poems on love which end by satirizing it or satirizing love-poetry, satirical poems which are translations. In fact twenty of the thirty-nine poems (counting the dedication) are more or less free translations; twenty-three are on love (though not all are love-poems); it is hard to class more than eight as strictly satirical (18, 20, 29, 31, 32, and 34-36), but there is gentle humour in almost all the others, with the exception of the dedication and 15-17. In the *Divers jeux rustiques* we must not expect to find a unified picture or a definitive conclusion.

*       *       *

It is perhaps surprising, after his outspoken comments in the *Deffence*, that Du Bellay's work as a translator produced some of his most beautiful poetry. In the preface to his first acknowledged translation, that of Book IV of the *AEneid*, published in 1552, he explains that, aware of the consoling power of poetry, yet lacking inspiration and depressed by illness and domestic problems, he sought solace in translating classical works. He was also aware that the *Deffence* had established him as an opponent of translation, especially that of poetry, although in fact his condemnation was largely of incompetent and frivolous translators. But his apparent volte-face was not as radical as it seems. In the *Deffence* he had distinguished between various methods of translation, and he maintained this distinction in later prefaces and letters. The difference is established by the

[43] 3-15 and 17 by Saulnier (*4*), who counts 'Au Lecteur' and 'A Monsieur Duthier' as pieces 1 and 2.

[44] The three poems which interrupt the neatness of the division, 14, 33 and 37, may have been placed where they are merely for the sake of variety. Helen O. Platt contends otherwise in 'Structure in Du Bellay's *Divers jeux rustiques*', *Bibliothèque d'Humanisme et Renaissance*, XXXV (1973), 19-37. But it would be odd if this volume had been so much more carefully structured than the *Antiquitez* or the *Regrets*.

key-words *traduction* and *translation*, used in a consistent
fashion by Du Bellay.[45] For him, *traduction* is a word-for-word
rendering suitable only for the communication of factual know-
ledge without any attempt to reproduce linguistic style or
beauty. *Translation* aims to convey as accurately as possible the
meaning and structure of the original, without restricting the
natural flow of the translator's language. *Imitation*, with which
much of the *Deffence* is concerned, is unlike either in that the
imitator is free to choose as much or as little of the original text
as he pleases, to divulge his sources or not as he wishes, and to
use them in whatever way he likes, thereby producing what may
justly be considered an original composition.

  *Translation* was clearly linked with Du Bellay's conception of
*imitation*, and certainly made more demands upon the poet's
creative abilities then did *traduction*. *Translation* was less an
attempt to produce a literal rendering of the original than an
attempt to convey its ideas and, at the same time, to produce in
the reader of the translation the very emotions and reactions
which a reader of the original would have experienced. For this
purpose, the poet might use paraphrase, transposition into con-
temporary terms, or compensation. The *translateur* can follow
the structure and presentation of the original ideas, imitating
grammatical and metrical constructions where possible; this will
almost certainly necessitate alterations of words and word-
order. He can translate the vocabulary as closely as possible;
then he may need to compose his own verbal structures so that
the French reads smoothly. He can disregard metrical
restrictions and the word-order of the original if the otherwise
resulting French would sound unnatural. 'Le translateur n'a
point malfaict son devoir, qui sans corrompre le sens de son
aucteur, ce qu'il n'a peu rendre d'assez bonne grace en ung
endroict s'efforce de le recompenser en l'autre' (*Le Quatriesme
Livre de l'Eneide ... par J.D.B.A.* (Paris, 1552), *épitre-préface*;
cf. Chamard, *1*, VI, p.250).

  The translation of the *Moretum*,[46] which opens the *Divers*

---

[45] See Margaret B. Wells, 'What did Du Bellay understand by "translation"?',
*Forum for Modern Language Studies*, XVI (1980), 175-85.

[46] For comparisons of detail, see Saulnier, *4*, pp.190-94, and M. Glatigny, 'Du

*jeux rustiques*, is an excellent example of transposition. The aim of the Roman author, wrongly thought in Du Bellay's time to have been Virgil, was evidently to accumulate realistic detail in order to build up a vivid picture of ancient Italian country life. Du Bellay seems to have had two aims in mind: firstly, as Ronsard so often did, to transform the setting and the characterization into something of immediate appeal to French people, and secondly, in contrast with Ronsard, to keep his style simple and discreet. The characters are made French in name, origin and description; thus Simylus becomes Marsault, with a 'petit jardinage' in place of a small field, and singing 'chansons de village', and the negress Scybale becomes the red-haired Limousin peasant Catou. Mythology and periphrasis are rejected; 'Volcanus Vestaque' become 'la tuyle et la braize', and the 'guttas olivi Palladii' are rendered simply as 'un peu d'olif'. Vocabulary is kept as straightforward as possible; although the principles of the *Deffence* might have suggested the neologism *nasitort* for the Latin 'nasturtia', Du Bellay favours the French 'cresson allenois'. Lines 125-30 evoke rapidity and precision of action, while bareness of description parallels economy of movement. The decasyllabic couplets run easily, achieving through *enjambement* a natural, flowing effect; only rarely is word-order sacrificed to rhyme and metre (25-26, 105-07). Certainly in Du Bellay's 'Morctum' poetic considerations play a prominent part, while absolute fidelity to the original text is of secondary importance.

Transposition also occurs in the 'Vœux rustiques', with their frequent references to Anjou and the Loire, but here it does not seem to be Du Bellay's main aim. He and Navagero are both subscribing to the pastoral convention, the notion that happiness and peace are to be found in the supposed simplicity and innocence of country life seen through rose-coloured spectacles. The countryman's emotions are presented as strong but pure, uncorrupted by social sophistication and competition; one senses that even the 'rigueur' of Thenot's sweetheart (poem

Bellay traducteur dans les *Jeux Rustiques', Information littéraire*, XVIII (1966), 33-41.

12) proceeds only from filial obedience. William Empson[47] explains how the pastoral convention nevertheless tolerates 'learned and fashionable language' worthy of its nobility; but, except in a few passages such as 2, viii and 3, i, Du Bellay's diction remains well below the level of Navagero's, deliberately reflecting the naïveté of his Angevin peasants. They make their prayers for good crops and fair winds, not in votive epigrams modelled on classical Greek and Latin, but in folk-songs only slightly stylized and elevated. Realistic details are added to Navagero's; Ceres and Pan are seen as vivid figures, fair-haired or goat-footed; Thenot trembles, his future mother-in-law eavesdrops, the winnower admits to 'ahaner' (Cotgrave, *23*: 'to keepe time with lowd sighes unto his toylesome strokes'); Thenot's 'arres' and the 'granges, greniers, celiers' of poem 5 are not in the Latin. Navagero uses the graceful elegiac metre, but Du Bellay is able to reproduce the content of each couplet in a seven-syllable quatrain in 2 and 4, in a six-syllable sixain in 3; 6, 7, 8, 9, 11 and 13 use the still more popular *rimes plates*.

As many appreciations have already shown (cf. *18*, *9*, pp.66-67, and on *vœux* in general, *24*, pp.296-305), it is poem 3, 'D'un vanneur de blé, aux vents', which outshines all the other *vœux*, perhaps all Du Bellay's other translations. Here the atmosphere is totally French, form and content are in perfect harmony, and yet the close relationship to the original is unmistakeable. The last stanza follows the Latin with fair accuracy, the first does so with still more; but the second is re-created to evoke an atmosphere familiar to the poet's readers. The choice of 'je' as subject eliminates the peasant Idmon, and makes the poem intensely personal; the general 'serta' and baskets of saffron are omitted in favour of specific flowers of the French countryside. Navagero gives lightness and airiness to his poem by short vowels and trisyllables, Du Bellay by feminine endings, both internally and at the rhyme, above all in the first stanza. In the third, the sounds of 'j'ahanne' and 'je vanne' convey the panting effort needed for the work. Du Bellay's poem is a blend of translation, adaptation and re-creation, so well put together that all harmonizes into a coherent and entirely satisfying whole.

[47] *Some Versions of Pastoral*, London: Chatto and Windus, 1935, p.11.

In similar vein to the translations from Navagero, and also linked to the pastoral and votive traditions, are the two free translations from the earlier Italian neo-Latinist Bembo; and comparable with these, in their alternation between literalness and freedom, are the two *baisers* translated, the first from Sannazaro, the second from Du Bellay's own Latin *Poemata* — unless the version there is a translation from his French. Completely different in style and approach is Du Bellay's re-working of the first hundred lines of Ovid's *Metamorphoses* IX, 'Le Combat d'Hercule et d'Acheloys' (pronounced, as line 24 shows, to rhyme with 'ceste fois'). Saulnier classes it as an ode (*4*, p.liii), but it is really an epic fragment in its stress on heroic action representative of all humanity. If the brisk line-length seems short for epic, yet the stanza-pattern forms a long and strong unit. One of Du Bellay's aims seems to have been to intensify the pictorial effect of the original; he has evidently in his mind's eye a vivid and exact picture of a bullfight (cf. *Regrets* 120 and 121). His opening, unparalleled in the Latin, is with the topos of preterition, 'passing over' a wide range of possible subjects to imply that his own is as great or greater, and to demonstrate his learning, versatility and power of close-packed allusion. Stanzas ii and iv show his skill in summarizing the Ovidian exposition; he rejects Achelous's first-person narrative, and steps back to give a balanced and objective account. Many of Ovid's phrases are translated literally, or almost so, but Du Bellay expands them by adding visual detail, as in lines 58-60, 81-84, 94 and 165-70. The elaborate grammatical structures of lines 141-54 are from Ovid, whose aim was less naturalism than play of clever rhetoric; but Du Bellay's seven-syllable lines give the insults force, and the successive stages and movements of the combat are rendered with staccato *epitome*. Line 180 forms Du Bellay's climax, after which two stanzas take the actors off stage with a crisp summary of sixteen Latin hexameters.

It is of course impossible to say much about avowed translations whose originals, the two *courtisane* poems by Pierre Gilbert, are not extant. It would have been in accordance with tradition for the nostalgic farewells of Gilbert's heroine to be composed in elegiac couplets; but from the relative leisureliness of Du Bellay's decasyllables (e.g. poem 34, lines 57-58) one may guess that often, as in the 'Moretum', he uses a whole couplet to render a single hexameter or pentameter. The Latin may perhaps be sensed behind the periphrases of 34, 1-4 and 35, 123-24, the abstractions of 34, 5-12 and 35, 25-32, and such exclamations as 34, 17 (the Virgilian 'æternum ... vale', *AEneid*, XI, 98). One can say with more confidence that the choice of such poems for translation, with their opportunities for topical and universal satire, vividly realistic vignettes and epigrammatic concision, is characteristic of the Du Bellay of the *Jeux* as of the *Regrets*. He does not seem to find much wit in the original of 34 or add much wit thereto, except for oxymorons as in lines 12 and 40 and the *pointe* of the final couplet; no French equivalent is substituted for the allusions in line 96. There is more sparkle in poem 35, with the word-play of lines 24 and 32, the sarcasm of 39-40, the pithiness of 44, 58 and 66, and another neat concluding couplet.

* * *

One could almost say that over half the *Jeux rustiques* are devoted to the portrayal of different aspects of love. In the four 'Vœux', despite the conceits of poem 13, one finds the pastoral ideal of innocent simplicity; a girl laments the imminent loss of her virginity; youths court their sweethearts by shy sequences of tears, prayers, the gift of a miniature and three kisses; two lovers, finally engaged, one senses, rather than married, promise each other a pure and eternal union of souls. The style and metre, as has been seen, are in conformity. The syntax is straightforward, making effects by simple repetition or parallelism; the twenty-eight lines of poem 14 even avoid all but two inversions. The rhymes are obvious and traditional ('blancheur ... frescheur', 'vœu ... nœu', 'visage ... image'), and the metaphors obvious and few ('lien', 'liant', 'arres'), apart from the symbolic flowers, bow and quiver, and picture.

A loftier and graver conception of love is to be found in poem 16, 'Chant de l'Amour et du printemps'. It is that which lay behind *L'Olive* and the 'Treize·sonnetz de l'honneste amour', although the sonnet form permitted only brief allusions to it;

and it was more fully expressed in Ode 3 of the 'Vers lyriques' of 1549, mentioned in Chapter 4. Love, said the ode, translating from Pontano,[48] is a divine force ruling all the world, which depends on the balance and harmony of the elements, as human communities depend on equity and peace, and nature on generation. Love, continued Du Bellay more independently, is just, loyal and honest; it is to be worshipped, thanked as the source of life and obeyed while life lasts. The graceful metre now known best as that of Ronsard's 'Bel aubépin' suggests the naturalness and delightfulness of this obedience.

The opening of the 'Chant' uses the same topos, Saulnier points out (*4*, p.36), as 'Le Combat d'Hercule'. This time, however, it provides a transition away from the subject of war to that of love. Love (stanza iv) is a greater force than Mars. It created the universe, as Du Bellay would have found from Plato's *Timœus*; a harmony of opposites and mutual attraction (stanzas v-vii) characterize this creation and are expressed in the music of the spheres. The keynote of a poem on such love, say stanzas viii-ix, should be a 'doulceur naïve', spontaneous and in accord with universal nature; and this tone dominates the choice of details, images, words and full sonorous vowels for the next nine stanzas. Love is lauded as irresistible (47-48), holy (54), delightful (55-56), inspiring (60), good, beautiful and pure (93-96). Although the poet can call it 'le seul plaisir de ma vie' (46), it brings with it 'mille sortes de plaisirs' (55): enthusiasm (60), springtime (61-68), the promise of harvest (69-72) and a Renaissance led by France (74-86). Yet the writer, a love-poet from his birth (91), returns to his chief concern (99-100), a pen-portrait of his mistress in which, as in Ronsard's 'Mignonne, allons voir ...', it is not her complexion which recalls a flower, but the flower which can only be seen as an image of her. All birds (157) are called as witnesses to the construction in her honour of a *locus amœnus*, an ideal pastoral beauty-spot, to be frequented by the Graces (192). In the penultimate stanza she is revealed still to be Olive, ranked once again with Laura, symbolized by laurel. The awed hush of the last stanza completes the

---

[48] C.H. Maddison, 'Sources of Du Bellay's *Les Louanges d'Amour*', *Modern Language Notes*, LXXIII (1958), 594-97.

devout eulogy of love more fittingly than did the shadowed close
of the 1549 ode.

Poem 17, the 'Chant de l'Amour et de l'hyver', was
deliberately written, at an unknown date, as a pendant to the
preceding 'Chant'. Not only are there verbal references (31-33,
87, 97-99, 187-90), but the structure is similar, with the opening
reference to the international military situation, the picture of
Love as a guiding god, the central digression which obliquely
compliments the King, and the final picture of the poet's tomb
in a *locus non amœnus*. It has the faults of a pendant, substi-
tuting Petrarchism for inspiration, and, for want of the latter,
returning to the *disperata* theme of ode 9 of the 'Vers lyriques'
of 1549 (as Du Bellay had already done in a 'Complainte' of
1552). Nevertheless, the conception of love as irresistible,
unchangeable and a completely absorbing obsession, conveyed
by the recurrent 'éternellement ... perpetuel ... tousjours ... sans
cesse', is consistent with the conception in the two eulogies of
love. Consistent also is the conception of chaste and honourable
love in poem 37, the 'Métamorphose d'une Rose', which seems
to be a compliment to some court lady recently widowed.

Though in the style of polite conversation rather than lofty
lyricism, the 'Elégie d'Amour' (poem 21), the 'Chanson' which
follows it and the 'Elégie amoureuse' (poem 33) put forward the
same view of love. Griffin takes the two elegies as illustrating
'the need poets felt for an underlying logical argument' (*12*,
pp.15-17), but in fact they make up with the 'Chanson' a triad of
logically argumentative love-poems, nothing unusual in an age
when Marguerite de Navarre's *Heptameron* had set a pattern for
literary debate on *questions d'amour*, to whatever extent she
reflects real-life discussions. In the 'Elégie d'Amour' the poet is
able to emphasize his sincerity (33-42), his Platonism (55-58), his
faithful and entire service (77-81, 113-14) and his Christianity
(83-86), while finding the opportunity for other allusions (12,
50-52), apt images (17-20, 68, 97-112), hyperbole (25-28) and
satirical quips (35-42), all neatly worked into the decasyllabic
couplets traditional in love-elegies.

Griffin (*12*, p.15) illuminates the first twenty-five lines of the
'Elégie amoureuse', but the rest is not as artless as line 19 claims;

it is a brief and basic account of Neoplatonism, perhaps straight
from Plato's *Symposium*. Love is inspired by the beautiful (line
26; *Symp.* 197 and 204), by the spirit even more than the body
(36; 210). Love is good (46; 196); beautiful (46; 197); the source
of all creation (47; 196-97); the source of virtue and glory (48-49;
178 and 208). Love seeks love as its counterpart (52-53; 191-92);
and virtuous love is lifelong (55-60; 183). By concise allusion,
the poet establishes on a firm basis of authoritative doctrine all
that has been said in poems 16, 21 and 22, and implied in 17, 37
and even the 'Vœux rustiques'.

However, Du Bellay could swing to the opposite pole, as in
the well-known poem 20, 'Contre les Petrarquistes', on which
Saulnier (*4*), Fucilla and Weinberg[49] have commented fully:

> J'ay oublié l'art de Petrarquizer ...

Saba (*14*, p.106) dismisses it as a 'momento d'umore'; but the
same satire of Petrarchist clichés is to be found in poem 18, 'De
sa peine et des beautez de sa dame'. This poem, 18, is in *vers
rapportés* (see p.25), exploring no fewer than five stock images,
introduced in lines 7-9 and each appearing in no fewer than
seven stanzas. Du Bellay gives an indication (as he does not in
poem 17) that this is satirical parody, in line 1's 'Il me plaist icy'
and perhaps in line 4's 'contr'imitée' instead of merely 'imitée'.
Further, the same unsubtle and fleshly conception of love is to
be found in the two *baisers* (poems 23 and 24), the two trans-
lations from Bembo (poems 25 and 26), and poem 14, the
'Villanelle'.

In form, poem 14 is not a villanelle in any strict sense, but a
*double ballade* of four stanzas, with the typical *abab*, *bcbc*
rhyme-scheme and a two-line refrain. This harks back to
Marotic metres; and indeed, although Saulnier ignores the
possibility and Chamard (*1*, V, p.27) saw only Ronsard's
influence, the poem is a frank pastiche of the songs of Clément
Marot. Although the Marguerite whom the latter most often

[49] J.G. Fucilla, 'Sources of Du Bellay's *Contre les Petrarquistes*', *Modern Philology*, XXVIII (1930-31), 1-11; B. Weinberg, 'Du Bellay's *Contre les Petrarquistes*', *L'Esprit Créateur*, XII (1972), 159-77.

addressed was the sister of François I, he gave that name to a
prostitute in his epigram 'D'Annette et Marguerite'. The
opening movement of Marot's 'Chant de May et de Vertu',
'Voulentiers en ce moys ici ...', is closely paralleled by that of
Du Bellay's 'Villanelle', while Du Bellay's poem's first line is
closer still to that of Marot's 'Chant de May', 'En ce beau moys
delicieux'. Du Bellay's stanza ii recalls such a song as 'O cruaulté
logee en grand' beaulté ...', his stanza iii imitates the *chanson*

> Puis que de vous je n'ay aultre visage,
> Je m'en vois rendre Hermite en ung desert

and the surprise ending of his stanza iv resembles those of
Marot's epigrams 'Du jour des Innocens' and 'Des cinq poinctz
en amours'. If 'la couleuvre' lies beneath Marguerite's beauty,
so it does beneath her lover's respectful despondency.

The key to Du Bellay's thought, unifying his two attitudes,
lies in the puzzling poem 19, 'A Olivier de Magni sur les per-
fections de sa dame'. The syntax and metre are simple, recalling
the positive approach of 'Sur un chappelet de roses'; the train of
thought is less simple. 'In your poetry', one may summarize it,
adding one's own italics, 'I *seem* to see the beauty of your lady;
sing of love while love *blinds* you; without this no one can write
of love. When I was in love I *imagined* myself tormented, and
the universe *seemed* to respond; now that the veil has been
removed, I cannot write love-poems. I was the first in France to
do so, and you are a worthy follower of mine; continue. But
what am *I* to do now that France (ignorantly) laughs at love-
poetry? Sing the praises of your patron, and of love while you
still feel it; the poet can handle every subject. If love is the
principle of the universe, he should write of love, and all other
subjects through the help of love; but beware of being
disillusioned like Epimetheus.' That husband of Pandora was
deceived in her and by the gods; is Du Bellay not merely
'demystifying the myths' (cf. Demerson, *24*, p.322) but implying
that all love is a deceiving illusion? In that case, why encourage
Magny to continue in it? Perhaps the possibility that one's god
may be deceiving one is a risk which the true devotee of love, like

Pascal's wagerer, has to take.

Certainly Magny has to be warned against 'legere foy' (line 238) both on his part and on that of his beloved. Deluded blindness in the lover and cold shallowness in the beloved, says Du Bellay in this and the preceding and following poems, produce Petrarchist poetry, pleasing when one is in the mood for it and merely amusing when one is not. 'Contre les Petrarquistes', for all its satirical tone, also contains a key passage, and it is not the often-quoted

> Le plus subtil, qu'en amour je poursuis,
> > S'appelle jouissance.

It is the second half of the following stanza, where every word must be given its full value:

> Vous souhaitter autant de bien qu'à moy,
> Vous estimer autant comme je doy,
> Avoir de vous le loier de ma foy,
> > Voila mon Androgyne.

The Androgyne, Plato's fancied primeval human being with two faces, four arms and four legs but a single head and body, represents for Du Bellay the perfect union of two hearts and souls. The real and realistic lover does not embrace pain to please his lady; he seeks equal well-being for her and for himself. He does not grovel before a lady placed on a pedestal; he sees her as she is and values her as she merits. And he must not be rejected by courtly or Petrarchist disdainfulness; the beloved has her own duty, to value him and reward him as he deserves. Only if love on both sides is as sincere, frank and equal as in the 'Baisers' can it be painted in the glorious colours of the 'Chant de l'Amour et du printemps'.

\*     \*     \*

There are various ways of assessing an author's satirical attitude; perhaps the best is to examine on the one hand the content of the work, on the other hand the author's approach or tone. A satirical work should contain at least one of three ingredients; two are topicality, dealing with people or events familiar to the reader, and realism, that is, truthfulness in portraying the nature, shapes and proportions of these, and often general or universal truth. Thirdly, satire implies the existence of a more perfect state of affairs, or an ideal striven after; the work should therefore state or imply a set of criteria by which the existing, inferior situation may be judged. Meanwhile, a satirical author must be motivated by either humour or indignation, or a mixture of the two; if by neither, the work will become an unemotional description or a sermon. Topicality, realism, criteria-based judgments, humour and indignation: for a work to be successfully satirical, at least one of the first three and one of the last two should be discernible.

In the *Regrets*, Du Bellay is topical, realistic, judging by clear criteria, and most often indignant. In the *Jeux rustiques*, tone and content combine in different ways to produce a variety of satirical and humorous verse. Very rarely is the satire as bitter or violent as in the *Regrets*; more often it makes gentle fun, as of the clichés of Petrarchism in poems 18 and 20. In the 'Complainte des Satyres', the two animal epitaphs, 'A Bertran Bergier' and the 'Hymne de la surdité', there is no intention of hostile satire against subject or dedicatee; only, in passing, satirical shots are fired, for example by the satyrs against the venality of 'toutes femmes'. Satire is more strongly directed against the Vieille Courtisane and her world and the Abbé Bonnet, more strongly still in 'Contre une vieille' and the 'Epitaphe d'un flambeau'; even so, it is softened by the fact that the last-mentioned poem concerns an abstract subject, and the three others describe imaginary though typical characters. Even when admitting satire into this volume, Du Bellay remembered that it was to be a book of 'jeux'.

In the two epitaphs on pet animals Du Bellay is humorously affectionate and realistic, if occasionally verging on fantasy. Following the well-established tradition of the descriptive *blason*, he gives a vivid portrait of the dog Peloton as a pretty and beloved pet, healthy and lively, but also well-bred and dainty, as is suggested especially by the negatives of lines 30, 43-46 and 54-55. Animal epitaphs were rarer than *blasons* were then, and rarer than such epitaphs are now. Lightly suggested anthropomorphism appears from the start in the very idea that a dog might have an epitaph, a tomb and an after-life, in the use of terms more appropriate to human beings ('barbelette', 'maintien riand' and 'maintien damoiselet') and in the fancies concerning Peloton's choice of 'exercice' and musical accomplishments (40-42). He is compared to his advantage with other dogs, animals (14, 104) and, by implication, humans (71-74). The light seven-syllable lines, crisp alliteration, especially of *t*, and mock-lofty classical allusions complete the picture.

The death of the cat Belaud is stated to have followed that of Peloton (175-80), and the later epitaph is clearly modelled on the earlier. Both realistic description and whimsical fantasy reappear, and many lines such as 129-46 and 153-56 are obvious reworkings. However, Du Bellay also shows an evident intention to vary his approach. The explicit parody of a sepulchral inscription which opens Peloton's 'Epitaphe' is replaced by echoes of the traditional *deploration*, even of the bereaved lover's *complainte* (7-8, 57-59), and of Du Bellay's own *disperata* poems. Where the dog wins immortality for his loveable nature, the cat wins it for his beauty (17-18, 55-56); there are numerous comparisons with precious materials, besides the impertinent one with the rainbow. The comparison of lines 97-98 is impertinent in a different and double-edged way, and is emphasized by the slowing down of the octosyllabic lines, which elsewhere move almost as lightly and rapidly as the heptasyllables. Lines 99-102 hint that Belaud's 'trongne ... bonne' was not his only point of likeness to the scholars of the Sorbonne.

Topicality and humour are seen in the two parodies of Petrarchist style, 18 and 20, in the 'Hymne de la surdité' and in 'A Bertran Bergier, poète dithyrambique'. The latter is a mock-eulogy of an old friend and fellow-student, to whom ode 6 of the 'Vers lyriques' was dedicated, and who had joined in the 'folastrissime voyage d'Hercueil'. One does not know how seriously Bergier aspired to the title of poet, but the three pieces of his which were discovered by Saulnier[50] are mere versification for amusement. Du Bellay quotes Greek legends with obvious inappropriateness, and evidently speaks only too truly of Bergier's lack of art, labour and study. Ironically, he praises Bergier for becoming a perfect poet without these aids or those enumerated by Sebillet (Saulnier, *4*, p.119), and recants his own statement in the *Deffence* that 'le naturel n'est suffisant à celuy qui en Poësie veult faire œuvre digne de l'immortalité' (*2*, II, 3, title). In lines 71-76, 'vol des oyseaux', 'bedonniques' and 'hachi-gigotis' refer precisely to two of the texts published in Saulnier's article; but Du Bellay deliberately reverses his descriptions of them, describing as 'rimes heroiques' lines which vary from five to eight syllables, as 'vers plus petits' lines which vary from ten to fourteen. Despite the friendly irony, he ends with a genuine compliment when he suggests that a poetaster can yet be a delightful companion.

The 'Hymne de la surdité' is a display of brilliant variety. Du Bellay is simultaneously taking up the Renaissance tradition of the paradoxical *declamatio*, exemplified in masterly fashion by Erasmus's *Encomium Moriæ*, and throwing his burlesque panegyric into the form, new in French, of a Ronsardian *hymne*. Ronsard's two volumes of gravely meditative eulogies of heroes and abstract concepts, in alexandrine couplets and learned lyrico-epic style, had appeared in 1555-56. Du Bellay burlesques Ronsard in his metre and diction, his opening use of the modesty topos exaggerated to the point of absurdity (lines 1-5), the pompous introduction of his subject (37-44), the meticulous scientific account of it (45-58), the pseudo-scientific debate on its value (61-86) and the final allegorical picture and mock prayer. His sincere compliments to Ronsard (7-12, 21-25, 143-51) make it clear that his parody and his occasional digs (26, 152-53) are innocent ones. There is real satire, however, in his hits at petty Italian sovereigns (6), unworthy clerics (14) and a worldly Pope (199-206), and in his sustained criticism of all the social abuses which strike the ear, balanced against a genuine appreciation of

[50] V.L. Saulnier, 'Des vers inconnus de Bertrand Bergier, et les relations du poète avec Dorat et Du Bellay', *Bibliothèque d'Humanisme et Renaissance*, XIX (1957), 245-51.

the positive benefits, less of deafness than of freedom and solitude.

Real satire, topical and critical, appears in the 'Epitaphe de l'Abbé Bonnet'. Bonnet is neither a genuine 'docteur de la Sorbonne' nor merely the traditional type of omniscient quack. The physical description of lines 65-72, though comically accumulating as many animal parallels as possible, builds up an individual portrait which might well have been recognizable to contemporaries; but if so, *pace* Chamard (*1*, V, p.111), one can guess with fair confidence that the name of the original was not Bonnet. A clue, perhaps even a gloss, may be found in Cotgrave's definition: 'Prendre le bonnet: To commence Master of Arts, ... to refuse, or have no need of, further tutoring' (*23*, *s.v.* 'bonnet'). Du Bellay paints a charlatan who has no right to the costume of a M.A. (83-86), but is confident in his own ignorance (1-18); as Saulnier explains (*4*, p.111), 'fors poëtes et orateurs' excludes all writers in prose as well as in verse, and 'sans loy, paragraphe, et chapitre' all ability to refer to them. But Bonnet's pretensions to knowledge are thoroughly up to date for the 1550s — his interest in Platonism and the Kabbala; in Hebrew, the original tongue of the Old Testament, and Italian, the source of the latest fashionable borrowings; in magic, alchemy and astrology, so much patronized by Catherine de Médicis. In these last fields he has, like many real-life Renaissance occultists, made a fortune out of his dupes (46-52), though his miserly habits prohibit any show (73-82). Perhaps inconsistent with these habits, and another hint that a real individual may be in view, is his passion for baseless litigation (59-60, 111-34). The final fact is his recent death (29-30, 108-10, 136-42); however traditional Du Bellay's jokes about this, they would have little point unless founded on fact. We seem to have in this poem a topical caricature very much akin to Du Bellay's earlier 'Satyre de Maistre Pierre du Cuignet' (*1*, V, pp.236-51).

'La Vieille Courtisane' continues the story begun in Gilbert's two poems, but is inspired also, as Chamard's edition shows, by many other sources, from Horace, Virgil and Ovid to Villon, Fernando de Rojas, Erasmus and Aretino, and by Du Bellay's own experiences in Rome. He credits his heroine with all the

accomplishments (43-46, 345-54) and the fashionable outfits and
accessories (171-78, 222-25) of a Roman courtesan; her exploits
at the peak of her career (357 ff.) are obviously a collection of
those attributed to real celebrities, as to Louise Labé in France.
Her fall into poverty-stricken old age is due to a combination of
causes, misplaced love as in Villon's 'Regretz de la belle
Heaulmiere', the use of witchcraft as in the *Epodes* and
*Eclogues*, the birth of a daughter at a date hardly compatible
with the indications of her own age, and the edict of Pope Paul
IV against prostitution. The final topoi, 'emotion prevents my
continuing' and the plea for a sympathetic hearing, go back to
old rhetorical tradition.

Despite this multiplicity of sources, Du Bellay's character-
ization is considerably more penetrating and integrated than
Gilbert's. The latter's courtesan lacks both character and clear
motivation for her first repentance, inspired only by 'Bon
Advis'. The Contre-Repentie shows more character; she knows
that her desires are 'vicieux' (35, line 6), but they, her 'vigour'
(10), and her wish for 'doulceur de ... vie' (11) and liberty (4)
are too strong. The Vieille Courtisane shows the same clear-
sightedness throughout her autobiography; she recognizes that
her regret is too late to be fruitful, her repentance too late to be
meritorious; her past life was a 'forfaict' (line 16), even if
foolishness (19) and upbringing (22) could be blamed for it;
other misfortunes were due to her capricious 'inconstance' (5,
54-58) and insistence on liberty (60-62, 71-82). Her contempt for
herself (115 ff., 273 ff., 326-36) is less than her contempt for her
lovers (89-106, 137 ff., 281 ff., 378-80). Her misfortunes spring
from her own character; even when they seem accidental
(109-12), the point is that she has let herself drift into a life
which is at the mercy of accident (517-18).

Every characteristic of satire appears in this poem: topicality,
realism and attention to detail which guard the portraiture from
becoming caricature, clearly implied criteria against which Du
Bellay measures his heroine and she measures herself, humour in
his portrayal of her and indignation in her portrayal of others.
The style and versification are also highly resourceful, with the
varied vocabulary, the concise and wide-ranging allusions, the

discreet but telling devices of rhetoric. The Vieille Courtisane shows much more quiet wit than in the translations from Gilbert, in the irony of lines such as 33-36, 47-48 and 86-88, and the ambiguity of 52 and 184. The decasyllabic couplets are less stiff than in poem 35, much less so than in 34; there was some *enjambement* there and more in the 'Contre-Repentie', but here it flows readily to convey emphasis, surprise or emotion, as in lines 17-19, 27-29 and 109-10.

Of the two poems which can be called indignant satire, 'Contre une Vieille' (see *18* on its sources) shows only mock-indignation; it is a caricature remote from reality, whose merits are its concise evocativeness, its varied constructions ('Tu es ...', 'Pour ...', 'Tu peulx ...', 'Par toy ...') each adroitly sustained throughout a sixain and changed in the next, and its surprise climactic-anticlimactic ending. In contrast, the subject denounced in the 'Epitaphe d'un flambeau' is real, topical, and so unedifying that the indignant poet refers to it only in the most enigmatic terms. Chamard (*1*, V, p.123) identifies it with Protestant heresy or its repression; Saulnier (*4*, pp.xlvii and 125), followed by Saba (*14*, pp.241-42), with prostitution; Helen Platt (*art. cit.* (note 44), p.30) with witchcraft. None of these suggestions explains all the mythological and historical allusions.

Careful observation of verb tenses and re-arrangement of the references in chronological order establish a sequence of events, and point to the solution of the enigma. It seems that Du Bellay centres the poem on the Franco-Spanish treaty of Vaucelles (Feb. 1556; lines 79-80); the breaking of the treaty (July 1556; 81-90); the subsequent invasion of Italy by the Duke of Alba (Sept.-Nov. 1556; 32-34); and the resulting forty-day truce between Alba and Paul IV (Nov. 1556; 97-99). The view that war and disease go hand in hand was commonly held, and the allusions to Byblis (66), Myrrha (68) and Pasiphae (71), not to mention the echo of Du Bellay's own poem 'L'Anterotique' (63-64), indicate that the disease is venereal. An examination of the more evocative descriptions in lines 41-43 reveals the disease to be syphilis. This identification is reinforced by the striking similarity between some parts of the poem and Fracastoro's

*Syphilis, sive morbus gallicus* of 1530.[51]

Despite the exaggerated invective, the brisk octosyllabic couplets often rhyming epigrammatically, and the final *pointe* based on the rhyme 'Paris ... Phalaris', Du Bellay's approach in this poem is deeply serious. It strikes harder and deeper than any other satire in the *Divers jeux rustiques*, as hard and deep as any satiric sonnet in the *Regrets*. Fracastoro saw syphilis as a divine punishment for mortals' *hubris*; Du Bellay is prepared to convict of *hubris* all those who are responsible for declaring and waging war. The poem is a *blason* only in form, an epitaph only in name. At a time of peace, Rome and Paris may think the scourge is dead; but the tomb of the first line 'couve les cendres' which are merely incubating until the time comes for them to break out again in horrible life. Here, as so often, Du Bellay shows his characteristic individuality of approach, renewing a traditional form and filling it with profound meaning.

[51] See Margaret B. Wells, 'Du Bellay and Fracastoro', *Modern Language Review*, LXVIII (1973), 756-61.

## Conclusion

On 2 January 1560, less than two years after the publication of the *Antiquitez*, *Regrets* and *Divers jeux rustiques*, Du Bellay was found dead at his working table from a stroke in the night.

One cannot attempt a summing up of his work as if any one or all three of the great collections were the climax and final presentation of it. They were the outcome of a period of his life disappointing and disillusioning for the man, but remarkably fruitful for the poet. But in 1558 and 1559 he published more translations, complimentary and ceremonial poems, and a substantial satire, 'Le Poete courtisan', pursuing and elaborating with deceptive mildness ideas to be found in *Regrets* 139-50. He also composed several long verse discourses on political and literary subjects, left among his papers at his death. Certainly one cannot say that his powers were declining after 1557.

At worst, he was pausing to leap forward again. Had he lived, he would surely have produced still more telling satires, still more accurate translations, and probably also more free imitations like those in the *Jeux rustiques*; he might also have gone on to still more pungently realistic love-poetry. He could hardly have survived at court without composing further official poetry; but he might well have approached this task with the originality of *Regrets* 177-89. If Gadoffre is right (see pp.44 and 76 above), he was planning a whole sequence or volume glorifying the French monarchy and its role in history. Gadoffre also suggests (*10*, *passim*) that he had the makings of a religious poet; he published a group of expressly Christian poems in 1552, and left a moving 'Hymne chrestien' and 'Ample discours au Roy' in 1560, while much of the *Regrets* and all the *Antiquitez* are basically religious in spirit. He might have surprised his readers, as in his Roman collections, by something almost totally new.

Du Bellay's work as it has come down to us represents great promise partially fulfilled. If his 'vers se trouvent imparfaits', yet he is 'seur à tout jamais de vivre' ('A Monsieur d'Avanson', lines 2 and 108).

Heureux, de qui la mort de sa gloire est suivie ...
                                                    (*Regrets*, 20)

# Select Bibliography

## EDITIONS

We refer to the first two editions, but the last four include useful notes.

1. *Œuvres poétiques*, édition critique publiée par Henri Chamard, Paris (S.T.F.M.), 6 vols, 1908-31. An extract from vol.V is published separately: *Divers jeux rustiques*, édition critique par Henri Chamard, Paris: Didier (S.T.F.M.), 1947.
2. *La Deffence et illustration de la langue françoyse*, édition critique par Henri Chamard, Paris: Didier (S.T.F.M.), 1948.
3. *Les Antiquitez de Rome et les Regrets*, avec une introduction de E. Droz, Geneva: Droz, Lille: Giard (T.L.F.), 1947. The poems are numbered as by Chamard.
4. *Divers jeux rustiques*, [nouvelle] édition critique commentée par V.L. Saulnier, Geneva: Droz, Lille: Giard (T.L.F.), 1947. Saulnier numbers the preface and dedication as 1 and 2; thereafter Saulnier's number for each poem is Chamard's plus 2.
5. *Les Regrets ... suivis des Antiquitez de Rome plus un Songe*, texte établi par J. Jolliffe, introduit et commenté par M.A. Screech, Geneva: Droz (T.L.F.), 1966. The poems in each sequence are numbered as by Chamard.
6. *L'Olive*, texte établi avec notes et introduction par E. Caldarini, Geneva: Droz (T.L.F.), 1974. Poems numbered as by Chamard.

## SELECTED CRITICAL WORKS ON DU BELLAY

7. Bellenger, Yvonne, *Du Bellay: ses 'Regrets' qu'il fit dans Rome*, Paris: Nizet, 1975. Emphasis on Du Bellay's different personae and styles, with 'documentative' extracts from his works and his contemporaries'.
8. Chamard, Henri, *Joachim Du Bellay (1522-1560)*, Lille: Librairie Le Bigot Frères, 1900. Seminal, largely reproduced in *21*.
9. Coleman, Dorothy G., *The Chaste Muse. A Study of Joachim Du Bellay's Poetry*, Leiden: E.J. Brill, 1980. The title is less of a *leitmotif* than is suggested; the emphasis is on Du Bellay's use of classical learning.
10. Gadoffre, Gilbert, *Du Bellay et le sacré*, Paris: Gallimard, 1978. Perhaps the most deeply penetrating study yet of Du Bellay's thought in the context of his time.
11. Gray, Floyd, *La Poétique de Du Bellay*, Paris: Nizet, 1978. A detailed analysis of Du Bellay's poetic techniques in the sonnet sequences.

12. Griffin, Robert, *Coronation of the Poet: Joachim Du Bellay's Debt to the Trivium*, Berkeley and Los Angeles: University of California Publications in Modern Philology, 96, 1969. Uses the techniques of Renaissance logic and rhetoric to illuminate many poems.

13. Marchi, Giovanni, *I Sonetti romani di Du Bellay*, Rome: Bulzoni, 1974. A 25-page essay followed by the text of the *Antiquitez*, selected *Regrets*, and the *Romae descriptio*, with Italian translations and interesting annotations.

14. Saba, Guido, *La poesia di Joachim Du Bellay*, Messina-Firenze: G. d'Anna, 1962. Well documented account of previous critics' comments, balanced by his own. Gives most attention to the *Olive*.

15. Saulnier, Verdun L., *Les Antiquitez de Rome*, Paris: Centre de documentation universitaire, 1950. A *cours de Sorbonne* on the *Antiquitez'* aim, background, content, sources, allusions and style.

16. ———, 'Commentaires sur les *Antiquitez de Rome*', *Bibliothèque d'Humanisme et Renaissance*, XII (1950), 114-43. Not a mere reworking of *15*; allusions of individual poems are pursued further and profitably.

17. ———, *Du Bellay, l'homme et l'œuvre*, Paris: Boivin, 1951; (*17a*) quatrième édition augmentée, Paris: Hatier, 1968. In the popular series 'Connaissance des lettres'; brief but well-packed. Perhaps too convinced of Du Bellay's inferiority to Ronsard.

18. ———, 'Sur deux poèmes des *Jeux rustiques* de Joachim Du Bellay', *Revue universitaire*, LIX (1950), 265-71. An elegant example of *critique des sources*.

19. Vianey, Joseph, *Les 'Regrets' de Du Bellay*, Paris: Malfère, 1930. Short, but goes wider than the title might lead one to expect.

## OTHER WORKS

20. Castor, Grahame D., *Pléiade Poetics. A Study in 16th-Century Thought and Terminology*, Cambridge University Press, 1964. Has transformed modern understanding of the Renaissance conception of imagination and imitation.

21. Chamard, Henri, *Histoire de la Pléiade*, Paris: Didier, 4 vols, 1939-40. After the introductory chapters, tends to treat each poet separately, but builds up a good total picture of each. Includes most of the content of *8*, updated to the year of writing.

22. Clements, Robert J., *Critical Theory and Practice of the Pléiade*, Cambridge, Mass.: Harvard University Press, 1942. Du Bellay figures with especial prominence in sections on sincerity, inspiration and the swan motif.

23. Cotgrave, Randle, *A Dictionarie of the French and English Tongues*, London, 1611. A dictionary by a 17th-century lexicographer with a fine understanding of Early Modern French and its use by writers.

24. Demerson, Guy, *La Mythologie classique dans l'œuvre lyrique de la Pléiade*, Geneva: Droz, 1972. The chronological approach and erudite detail may make it difficult to appreciate his masterly grasp of classical mythology and what it meant to the Pléiade.

25. Huguet, Edmond, *Dictionnaire de la langue française du seizième siècle*, Paris, 4 vols., 1925-67. Concentrates on words, senses and usages too late for Godefroy's *Dictionnaire* and too early for Littré's, with a wide range of supporting quotations.

26. Joukovsky, Françoise, *La Gloire dans la poésie française du XVI^e siècle (des Rhétoriqueurs à Agrippa d'Aubigné)*, Geneva: Droz, 1969. Stresses Ronsard's poetry, but includes an extensive and penetrating analysis of the *Antiquitez*.

27. Laumonier, Paul, ed., *Pierre de Ronsard, œuvres complètes*, Paris: (S.T.F.M.), 18 vols, 1914-67. The indispensable annotated critical edition of Ronsard's works.

28. McFarlane, Ian D., *A Literary History of France. Renaissance France 1470-1589*, London: Benn, 1974. A very thorough survey of the literature of the sixteenth century, with its historical and cultural background. Devotes 13 pages to Du Bellay.

29. Merrill, Robert V., and R.J. Clements, *Platonism in French Renaissance Poetry*, New York University Press, 1957. Good study of Platonic themes in Du Bellay and others of the Pléiade. 'In Du Bellay's mind Petrarchizing and Platonizing meant much the same thing.'

30. Raymond, Marcel, *L'Influence de Ronsard sur la poésie française (1550-1585)*, Paris: Champion, 1927. An important chapter concluding 'que Du Bellay n'est pas seulement le débiteur de chef de la Pléiade, mais un peu aussi son créditeur'. Many judicious remarks.

31. Vianey, Joseph, *Le Pétrarquisme en France au XVI^e siècle*, Montpellier: Coulet, 1909. Du Bellay was original, but not always as he claimed to be.

32. Weber, Henri, *La Création poétique au XVI^e siècle en France de Maurice Scève à Agrippa d'Aubigné*, Paris: Nizet, 1955. Good background information in first three chapters, followed by detailed study of principal themes of Pléiade poetry. Great sensitivity to individual poems.

33. Wells, Margaret B., *Du Bellay: a bibliography*, London: Grant & Cutler, 1974. Includes over 1,000 items published up to 1973.

# CRITICAL GUIDES TO FRENCH TEXTS

*edited by*

Roger Little, Wolfgang van Emden, David Williams